YOU CAN MAKE IT

SELLING REAL ESTATE

Other Books by Richard Steacy

Canadian Real Estate 7th edition 1987

Land Titles Registration in Canada and the USA

You Can Beat Inflation With Real Estate

Steacy's Practical Canadian Mortgage Guide

Listing and Selling Real Estate in Canada

A Practical Canadian Mortgage Guide
3rd edition 1986

YOU CAN MAKE IT

SELLING REAL ESTATE

RICHARD STEACY

Stoddart

First published in 1988 by
Stoddart Publishing Co. Limited
34 Lesmill Road
Toronto, Canada
M3B 2T6

CANADIAN CATALOGUING IN PUBLICATION DATA

Steacy, Richard, 1919-
    You can make it selling real estate

ISBN 0-7737-2245-9

1. Real estate agents.   2. Real estate business.
3. House selling.   I. Title.

HD1382.S76 1988   333.33'023   C88-094707-1

Printed and bound in the United States

To my sons,
Charles Richard Graham Steacy
William Harold Denham Steacy,
and their mother, Mary,
my wife

Contents

Preface

In 1977 I wrote a book titled *Listing and Selling Real Estate in Canada*.

That book contained highlights of twenty years' practical experience as a licensed real estate agent. This new book contains the best of that volume, plus another ten years' experience.

Plus a lot of recent research most agents would not have in their background.

There are two things I stressed in the foreword to *Listing and Selling*, which I repeat here:

Would it surprise you to know that a real estate agent does not sell real estate? If the listing contract between the vendor and agent is described as an "exclusive authority to sell," it can only be considered by the author to be a very loose interpretation of the nature of the contract.

The real estate agent's authority is basically limited to introducing potential buyers to the property, and hopefully producing one who is ready, willing and able to conclude a contract of sale between the buyer and seller; the seller being the vendor, and not the agent.

If the agent were to sell the property, he would logically have to have a power of attorney to do so. An agent cannot sell something he does not own.

If the foregoing appears to be slicing it a little thin, it is simply to illustrate how loosely we, as agents, are prone to accept what is not so, simply through years of common, ordinary usage. So when I write about "selling" you know what I mean. Right?

Secondly, when we refer to our client, who are we talking about? The one who is paying us, that's who! Sometimes we forget this.

If, for example, you are a sub-agent presenting an offer through the listing agent, do not refer to the buyer as your "client." Your client is the vendor, the one who is paying the listing agent. The only time a buyer can be considered to be a client is when the buyer is doing the paying, which occasionally happens.

If there is one word in the English language to ensure an agent's success, the word most surely would be *persistence*.

Apply the guidelines in the following pages with persistence, and I am sure you will succeed.

To qualify for my provincial salesman's licence thirty years ago, I filled out a form in a government office, provided proof of future employment with a broker, paid a modest sum of money, and I was on my way. The real estate board provided five morning lecture sessions for the basics; the broker paired me with an old pro, and away we went.

How times have changed. . . .

My first deal was a disaster. The lady of the house really didn't want to sell—I am convinced that all she wanted was a parade of visitors to while away her lonely hours. I came up with a buyer and my partner took the vendor to her lawyer's office where the deal was consummated.

My poor partner. He and his wife shopped in the same food store as the lady, and every time she saw them, she would holler to my partner in a loud voice that he was the crook that "stole my house."

My second deal was another lulu. I had an acceptable offer drawn and signed that contained a small open second mortgage. My partner was to meet me at the builder's house early in the morning with our deal, but before I left for work, the purchaser phoned to say he didn't want the second mortgage. Well, I scratched it out and presented the offer, requiring the vendor to initial the scratching. My partner had a fit, pointing out that since the second mortgage was open, we should have left it alone and it would have been ignored on closing.

When we went to get the purchaser to initial the scratches on the accepted offer, he said he had changed his mind about the whole thing. After two near heart attacks and a bit of work, he finally was persuaded to go along with it and we had the deal.

Reflecting on it though, I was probably right in doing the scratching. After all, I had to follow the instructions of the buyer.

It was a shaky start, but I plugged away, persisted, got involved and learned all I could. And after thirty years, I am still learning. No one will ever know it all about real estate, although I am sure some really think they do.

There have been some shady apples in the barrel, but generally speaking I believe that Canada's real estate agents, compared to some of the people we deal with, are basically like the soap, 99 and 44/100% pure. I suppose some of the cleanliness is caused by the fact that there are a lot of people and governments breathing down our necks all the time, but most of it is because of the wills of the agents just to do the best they can with what they've got, provide a decent living for their loved ones, remembering that they are living on a two-way street. The real baddies in my experience have been the buyers and sellers, the public.

Like people who use us, then sneak around behind our backs to the vendor to try and make a deal without benefit of the agent. The vendor who works with such a person, in my opinion, is just as bad as the other guy, and I consider it all to be a form of theft——stealing my commission.

Like people who won't pay the balance of a commission after we have worked our rear ends off moving their bricks and mortar.

Like people who want us to present conditional offers with a hundred in trust to be returned if the deal doesn't go——with some sneaky clauses in the deal. Nothing for the agent.

Like people who pick our brains and then sell privately.

It goes on and on, but with experience we learn to live with it and spot the jerks. We've all met a few. But the agent with any sense will close the books on a sour deal, call it a day and take tomorrow in stride looking forward to another whack at the brass ring.

It is not an easy business, this real estate business. No sinecure.

Whenever I get whacked by a potential vendor complaining about a 5 or 6 per cent commission, I take quiet delight in asking how much I will be paid if the property doesn't sell. Surely I'm entitled to something for my time if I fail to move the property. If 40 per cent of the M.L.S. listings sell and 60 per cent don't, at 5 per cent, that means that we are averaging a 2 per cent commission on all listings. The sales pay for the no-sales. And have you noticed that the ones who scream the loudest are usually the ones who want a pie-in-the-sky price?

Well, after all these years I am still at it. Sometimes I think an agent would be better off if he turned in his licence and wheeled and dealed as a private citizen. With our knowledge we could really shake it up.

I'll never forget the day the old cop on the beat poked his head in my office and asked me if he should buy a little piece of land he heard about. Without hearing a word he said, I said "Sure, sure, it sounds like a great deal." About a year later, I met him on the street and he told me that he had "taken my advice," bought the land, sold it about ten months later and made $17,000. Then he said, "Do you think I did good?"

Did good? Hell, we are so busy creating wealth for others that we never seem to have time for piling it up for ourselves. So read the chapter "Remember Number One" and make it pay.

I sincerely hope you make your pile, and if this book helps a little, I shall be very pleased.

Part One

THE SALESMAN

1

What Chance Have You Got in the Jungle?

A journal published by the Toronto Real Estate Board noted that "four out of every five people who try their luck at selling real estate eventually run out of luck."

The basic reason for this is that so many people "try their luck" at it.

There is very little luck attached to a licence to trade in real estate.

Passing provincial examinations does not mean one will be provided with any assurance of success in the real estate business.

Some come into the business with built-in talent. Sheer force of personality, drive, ambition and the will to be successful is part of it.

A more important part is energy. Energy to think nothing of working ten-hour days, non-stop, without making a dime.

How to direct this energy is the key.

There is an old truism in business that is particularly true for real estate agents——plan your work, and work your plan.

There is no point in going to the office in the morning, full of energy, if you are going to sit at your desk and say to yourself, "What'll I do today?"

You should know what you are going to do the day *before* you do it. Plan your work.

And tomorrow, work your plan.

The financial rewards that are possible in real estate will stagger you. Some agents consistently move more than $10- to $20-million worth of real property a year—— year after year after year.

They are not the ones who twiddle their thumbs wondering "What'll I do today?"

Going into real estate? Just thinking about it? This book will definitely help you.

You provide the energy, your broker and your real estate board will provide the training and continuing education, and I'll give you a helping hand right here.

Go for it.

2

The Salesman's Attitude

The days of the old, fast-talking, slippery salesmen are obsolete. If you follow the ground rules I have laid down in this chapter, you cannot help but be the better for it.

Take the word salesman. Look at each letter in the word and imagine that they represent the following words: Sincerity, Ability, Logic, Energy, Self-control, Manners, Amiability, Name.

Now see what some of the greats have said on the subjects.

Sincerity

Sincerity is to speak as we think, to do as we pretend and profess, to perform what we promise, and really to be what we would seem and appear to be.

John Tillotson (1630-94)
Archbishop of Canterbury

When you have a prospect in your car, what are you thinking about? The possible sale? Naturally. But before you get to the point of a possible sale you have to spend some time with the prospect, and this is where a glib tongue is going to get you in trouble and lengthen the distance between success and failure with the prospect. If the prospect is new at the business of associating himself with real estate salesmen, possibly through the potential purchase of his first home or investment, you will frighten him with a lot of blah blah and you will not gain his confidence. If he is an old pro at talking about real estate, your blah blah won't impress him one bit. So be sincere. Being sincere also means being truthful. It's nice to use a little varnish in life once in a while, but before we apply the varnish the surface should be smooth and free of impediments. Get the ground work straight, present the straight, honest facts about the property, good and bad; let your prospect know he is dealing with someone who is sincere in attempting to present a true, clear picture of

the property. Don't assume anything about the prospect.
Let him come to his own conclusions during the presentation. Once the facts have been made clear, then you can go
into the details and advantages of why the man should buy
what you are offering him. The real estate sale is not a hit
or miss affair, or a one shot deal. Not many prospects buy
the first property you show them. So remember, you are
competing with other salesmen. Let *them* scare him away.

Ability

*Men are often capable of greater things than they
perform. They are sent into the world with bills of
credit, and seldom draw to their full extent.*

Horace Walpole (1661-1724)
English author

Being a real estate salesman means having the compe-
tence, aptitude, talents, faculty, skill, power and capacity
to work with a multitude of subjects. An example is
zoning. This is the imposition of specific limitations on
the use of land and the construction and use of buildings
in a defined section of a municipality. It is very important
to understand it. I remember a very embittered lady who
was selling her house. She told me that she bought it to
use as a child day-care centre. The salesman who sold her
the property told her the particular section of the city in
which the house was located was zoned to allow such an
operation, and she believed him. He told her a half-truth.
It *was* zoned that way all right, but the child day-care
centre could be operated only in a building that was
specifically constructed for that purpose.

This sort of salesmanship is inexcusable. Don't let it
happen to you. Know your zoning.

Every time you list a property for sale you should
thoroughly investigate the zoning. What is its present
legal use? What could you do with the property? If the
building were demolished, what could you erect on the
site? These are not difficult facts to ascertain, but they are
important.

Zoning has a great bearing on land values regardless of
the present use of the structure. I had a case where I was

driving a client back to his office, and on the way he pointed to a modest three storey apartment building and said it was his. Next to the apartment building were three houses. I knew that people had tried to purchase the houses and couldn't afford them because of the zoning restrictions as to the size of a building you could construct. It immediately occurred to me that my client's building had been erected *before* the present zoning by-law, and his small building wasn't utilizing the full building allowance of the zoning. It would not be economical to demolish his building, but what he did do was purchase the three houses, which he was able to do because he added his already unused allowance for his present adjoining property to the allowance he legally had on the site of the three houses. He now owns a very nice thirty-five suite building in a very desirable area, right next door to his older one. One superintendent looks after them both. It all came about because I just happened to know and understand zoning.

If you know your zoning, believe me, it will add to your income, which is why you are in business.

Another important area is arithmetic. If you are slow in this department, get additional training by attending night classes or obtaining private tuition. It is better to start right from scratch, because you have probably forgotten a great deal about the fundamentals of the subject. Here are two simple questions; see how fast you can answer them. If you can't do them in your head, you need a refresher course.

(*1*) I invest $15,000 in a property that nets me $2,250 yearly. What is my return (%) on investment?

(*2*) I am paying $1,860 per year rent. This represents a 6 per cent net return on the lessor's investment, which would be what?

You don't have to be a whiz at it, but you should know the basics. I met a real estate salesman one day who had been selling for years. He did *not* know how to establish the unpaid principal balance of a fully amortized loan at any given year, despite the fact that he always carried with him a 224 page book showing monthly amortization tables. The answer to his problem was clearly outlined in the back of his book under a few charts of loan progression. He never bothered to look in the back of the book. He was not a very successful salesman. Play with arithmetic. Doodle with it. Obtain quick finding charts and tables and keep them handy.

Your ability is your responsibility. Learn all you can about your business. Study your provincial and municipal laws, and your real estate board rules. Don't feel discouraged if your manager is obviously lacking in his own knowledge of the business. Work somewhere else. Once I went to a great deal of trouble and a bit of expense obtaining interest factor tables, tailor-made to suit real estate. I had several copies printed and gave one to my manager. He brushed it aside saying, "What good is that?" *Everything* you can learn about your business is helpful.

If you are constantly alert and learning, learning, learning all the time, you will amass an enormous fund of automatic facts at your fingertips. You won't use them all the time, but they will be there when you need them, and you will always have that edge on the competition.

Logic
It was a saying of the ancients, that "truth lies in a well," and to carry on the metaphor, we may justly say, that logic supplies us with steps whereby we may go down to reach the water.

Isaac Watts (1674-1748)
English divine and hymn writer

Logic is the science of reasoning. You use it every day in the most mundane things you do. It has been said that the basic difference between a monkey and mankind is that a monkey does not have the power of reasoning. He apes things very well. Don't be a monkey in your business; logic will save you a lot of time.

Young couples love looking at new houses, regardless of their bank balances. If you are holding "open house" in a $200,000 home and in walks a young couple after hopping out of their ten-year-old jalopy, what do you do? Do you look at them and go back to the racing form? Be logical. Reason.

- They *are* looking at houses.
- If this one is too much for them, you could possibly steer them into a more reasonable deal to suit their resources.
- The jalopy could be there because the young couple are *saving* their money, not because they haven't got any.

Talk to them. Be friendly. Remember, you are the one who is supposed to know the business. How long have they been married? Both working? Renting? Living at the in-laws? Looked at many houses? A little probing will do wonders, and produce sales.

I well remember a Cadillac and Oldsmobile dealer telling me about one of his salesmen. A man walked into the showroom, looked at a snappy Cadillac convertible and asked the "salesman" how many miles he could get to the gallon with the car. The salesman looked at him and said, "If you have to ask that question about a car, you'd better look at an Olds 88 over here." The man turned to another salesman and repeated the question. The second salesman was logical. He realized that the man obviously must have had some reason for asking the question, and whatever the reason, it required an answer, so he promptly answered the question and just as promptly sold the man the Cadillac.

Don't try to play a guessing game with people when you are selling. Ask questions, and be logical and orderly in your mind about what the answers could or could not mean. If a man is speaking to you about investments, for instance, qualify him quickly by asking him *how much money he would like to invest*, not *how much money he has*. The latter is none of your business. The former is.

When you are listing properties for sale, one of your first logical questions should be "Why are you selling?" Quite often the reason for selling can be more important than the price. I'll take an over-priced listing any day if I know the owner is moving to Shanghai in six weeks.

Be orderly in your thinking, and this will automatically produce logic.

Energy

*Energy will do anything that can be done in the world;
and no talents, no circumstances, no opportunities will
make a two-legged animal a man without it.*

> Johann Wolfgang von Goethe (1749-1832)
> German philosopher and dramatist

This is inherent to successful salesmen. They thrive on
it. The following salesman's report card on one day's work
is a little extreme, but illustrative of how to fail.

9:10 Got up.
9:30 Dressed, listened to news.
10:00 Arrived at office, glanced at paper.
10:15 Had coffee with the boys, discussed last night's
TV shows.
11:00 Looked over listings other agents brought in (no
good).
11:30 Called friend and made date for dinner and drinks.
11:45 Called 3 prospects (nothing doing).
12:00 Out for lunch with the gang.
1:30 Haircut.
1:55 Stopped to supervise manhole operations in street.
2:00 Argued with foreman about moving my car.
2:30 Back at office.
2:45 Coffee break. Read paper. Like to know what's
new.
3:15 Argued with client about his lack of knowledge
about real estate. Real dumb cluck.
3:30 Criticized wording in offer being prepared by agent
next to me. He's new at the business.
3:45 Double-checked on date.
4:00 Nothing doing today so went home. Tough day.
Can't understand how that dumb guy next to me
had two sales last week.

The expression "go-go" must have been swiped from
observing successful salesmen at work. They really go-go.
They plan their day's work the night before; then work
their plan. When the alarm goes off they put 'er in high
gear and are on the job looking forward to a good hard
day's work. Their energy is boundless. It is directed.

They know the secret of getting started, and it is really very simple. The best way to do anything is *do it*. To illustrate this, if you are, for instance, going to do some cold canvassing on a street, you might find yourself sitting in your car thinking about it. You simply mechanically open the door, get out, walk up to the first house and knock on the door. Once you have performed this mechanical act you have found yourself forced into a situation because someone is going to answer that door and you are going to have to speak to him or her. The next knock will be easier, and shortly you will find yourself working with a head of steam.

Remember always that selling time is money. You only have so many hours in each day to earn your living, and one of the dangers about real estate is your freedom. You are free to knock off for a couple of hours any time, or a couple of days, or a couple of weeks. But you only hurt yourself and your family if you abuse this freedom.

If you are sitting in the office with an hour's break ahead of you, use it. Get on the phone. Talk to people. Talking is energy. Keep talking; your tongue will last as long as you will. Use your working hours productively. Do your paperwork and studying at night, when you must plan your next day.

If you put in a good, hard, constructive, honest day's work, you will feel better when you get home. You won't feel that you or anyone else has been cheated. You owe it to yourself and your family.

Self-control
It is the man who is cool and collected, who is master of his countenance, his voice, his actions, his gestures, of every part, who can work upon others at his pleasure.

Denis Diderot (1713-84)
French author

Some people, unfortunately, just do not understand the meaning of this, and probably never will. Self-control is:
- Keeping quiet when someone else is explaining something to a group of people when he obviously knows less about the subject than you do

- Keeping your temper when your client's little darling drips her ice cream cone on your car upholstery
- Restraining yourself when a potential purchaser is argumentative, bellicose, loud and has B.O.
- Swallowing your pride when your boss sounds off because he thinks you muffed a sale and you know he is wrong
- Patiently waiting for a late client to keep an appointment, when you "know" he is going to be a no-show
- Smiling when you lose a sale because you sincerely felt the vendor was too greedy
- Being cheerful when your competitor beats you out in obtaining a listing——and sells it.

How is your self-control? When was the last time you flew off the handle? Was it worth it? Did it impress anyone? You have to impress people in selling, so easy does it.

Manners

There is a policy in manners. I have heard one, not inexperienced in the pursuit of fame, give it his earnest support, as being the surest passport to absolute and brilliant success.

Henry Tuckerman (1813-71)
American art critic and author

Your carriage, bearing, conduct, deportment and polite, decorous behavior can be wrapped up in a neat parcel called manners. No one ever had to apologize to anyone for having good manners. I would like to remind you of a few quotations on the subject:

Good manners is the art of making those people easy with whom we converse; whoever makes the fewest persons uneasy, is the best bred man in company. ——Swift

Always behave as if nothing had happened no matter what has happened!——Arnold Bennet

Cultured and fine manners are everywhere a passport to regard. They are the blossom of good sense and good feeling. ——Samuel Johnson

Good manners are made up of petty sacrifices.
——Emerson

Manner is one of the greatest engines of influence ever given to man.——Whately

Nothing is more reasonable and cheap than good manners.——Anon

Good manners are a part of good morals, and it is as much our duty as our interest to practice both.——Hunter

Manners easily and rapidly mature into morals.——Mann

There is no policy like politeness, and a good manner is the best thing in the world either to get a good name, or to supply the want of it.——Bulwer

In manners, tranquility is the supreme power.——2nd wife of Louis XIV

Amiability
Amiable people, though often subject to imposition in their contact with the world, yet radiate so much of sunshine that they are reflected in all appreciative hearts.

Madame Deluzy (1747-1830)
French actress

When I was a student salesman, I once tagged along behind a co-worker as he was showing a couple through a house. The prospect wanted to have a few notes jotted down as he talked, and my friend handed a pen and piece of paper to the man. I was puzzled by this gesture, and thought my fellow salesman should have done the jotting. It wasn't until months later that I realized why he had done it. He couldn't spell c-a-t. This man was a whiz. A top producer. He had an IBM mind. He was extremely successful because of his one outstanding trait. He was one of the most amiable and immediately likeable men I have ever known.

He was one smart cookie. He knew he didn't have all the fine formal education of his competition, so he made use of the one great asset he had that shone like a beacon. To be amiable is to make us unwilling to disagree with those with whom we are on harmonious terms. That's what he did. If he ever felt like disagreeing on a point, he would sidestep it and go on to other features about the property.

This is a difficult mode of deportment for some of us, but I know a salesman who worked hard at it by smiling all the time. My, how that man smiled, and if you didn't have to look at it all day, it was all right.

So try your best to be agreeable. Give a little on the little points; it will give you some glue for the bigger ones. Don't be a nitpicker about details; leave your grouch at home and go to the office armed with a beaming, happy personality. I had a boss once who used to come charging into the office glaring and snorting like a bull every morning. He apparently thought this was the way to get people steamed up for a good day's work. I still remember him as a snorting bull.

Name

A good name lost is seldom regained. When character is gone, all is gone, and one of the richest jewels of life is lost forever.

Joel Hawes (1789-1867)
American clergyman

The last of our letters, but one of the most important. A person's name.

I remember driving past a man who was hammering on a For Rent sign. I stopped and asked him if I could help him lease the property. During our conversation, he began cursing the name of an acquaintance of mine, repeating that he was a crook. I didn't press the subject and left. Later in the day, I phoned my acquaintance and told him there was a man running around town telling everyone he was a crook. He asked me who said it, and when I told him, he said, "Aw, forget it."

That's what he thought of *his* name. Protect yours, it's the only one you have.

In the opera *Aida*, Aida was the daughter of the King of Ethiopia. Sales forces the world over have taken her name, but not in vain, to illustrate four successful steps to sales.

A   attention   (get it)
I   interest   (arouse it)
D   desire   (create it)
A   action   (sell it)

Good luck. It is no sinecure.

I expect to pass through this world but once. Any good therefore that I can do, or any kindness that I can show to any fellow creature, let me do it now. Let me not defer or neglect it, for I shall not pass this way again.

> Stephen Grellet (1773-1855)
> Quaker of French birth.
> Also credited to Emerson, John Wesley,
> William Penn, Thomas Carlyle.

Memorize it, and try it on for size.

3

Getting the Listing

The basic reason we are in business is to make money. This part of our business is soft-pedalled, and the reason is very obvious. If an agent attempted to replace a private sign with a realtor's sign by saying "Mr. Smith, for selling your home for $200,000 we will charge you $10,000," the private sign would stay where it is.

That is why we talk in percentages. It is much easier on the vendor's nerves to say the fee (or commission) will be five or six percent, rather than $10,000!

Here are some proven means of obtaining listings and getting those $10,000 deals.

Private "For Sale" Advertisements

The most obvious reason for attempting a private sale is to save money—the realtor's fee. Sometimes the price has been established in the owner's mind by hit-and-miss estimates of what can be learned from comparable neighborhood sales, but more often it is established by asking an agent or two for an opinion. Free, of course.

An agent, in responding to an advertisement, must have a happy and sincere telephone manner; one that will keep the advertiser on the telephone long enough to make an appointment to see the owner personally, and the property.

Don't get into a long-winded discussion at this stage. Just make the appointment, and take it from there.

Expired Listings

Ninety per cent of property owners whose listings have expired are unhappy, disillusioned and sometimes disgruntled. The property was for sale, and it didn't sell!

The other 10 per cent aren't really unhappy. They were just testing the market with overpriced listings, which of course is the most basic reason for *all* expired listings. Too much money (a combination of the price, terms and downpayment).

Stick to expired listings in your own area, where you are an authority on market value. Make an appointment to see the vendor personally and go armed with a cheerful outlook and comparable recent sales.

If an agent has been actively showing another broker's listing, and it expires, it is quite possible the agent has shown more interest and action in the property than the listing broker—which is a great opener to get the listing.

Remember. Don't try to do it on the telephone. Use the telephone to make an appointment and get to the owner.

Direct Mail

Don't swamp a neighborhood with "dropped mail" addressed to the "homeowner" asking for a listing. A mailing piece should be brief, and it should contain a message.

A powerful message is one that says we sold Nos. 4, 14, 27 and 56 Main Street last month. Main Street around the corner that is.

Or one that tells about the buyers left over after the agent sold No. 22.

Or one that introduces an agent as the one who sold $600,000 in the area last month.

Or one that tells how the broker can help the homeowner.

Pick 100 names and addresses from a directory *in your territory*. Address the mail by *name*. Five days after the mailing, make 100 telephone calls over the next five days.

Do this twice a month.

Individual House Builders

There are two reasons for a builder to construct a house. He is building it under contract, or he is building to sell.

Walk right onto the job site, inspect the house and speak to the builder. Not the plasterer. The builder.

After you have admired his workmanship, introduce yourself. Ask if its okay to show the house to a good client who is looking for a new house.

When you get *that* door opened, you turn in an open listing. Once you have shown the house, ask for an exclusive listing. A bit of good rapport here could make you a few thousand dollars.

Remember the house *will* be sold. By someone.

Private For Sale Signs

Here you have the two basic elements in a listing right in front of you: the owner and the property.

The only thing standing in your way is a sign.

Timing is very important. If you knock on the door before 10 a.m. you might find a grumpy owner trying to get down the first cup of coffee, and you'll be back in your car lickety-split.

Don't call at lunch time. Probably feeding the kids. Ditto for dinnertime. Make it between 10 and 11 a.m., 2 to 4 p.m. or 7 to 9 p.m.

Get the owner's name from a directory, or neighbor, and *use it*. People like the sound of their own name.

Knock on the door. Smile, introduce yourself, hand the owner your card and *step back one pace*. Nobody likes to be crowded.

Ask if you may inspect the house. This is very basic, so come right out with it before you say anything else.

During your inspection in the presence of the owner, slip in this question in your stream of kind remarks about the house——"What's your asking price?" The owner will usually blurt it out.

If you don't ask, the homeowner will start pumping you for a figure, which will be a free opinion of value. It is important to get the owner's price *first*.

If you can't get a listing, try to at least get an open listing, which will give you rapport with the owner. Show some action, then tighten it up.

Door Knocking

Cold canvassing is a great means of giving a new agent confidence, courage and experience.

It is a fact that some agents are nervous about knocking on a door because they are afraid that someone will answer, and the agent fears he will be in over his head.

A new agent must remember that the homeowner doesn't know he just got his licence last week and hasn't a clue about the property's value.

The basic reason for cold canvassing is to create rapport with the neighborhood homeowners. You will be a rare exception if a doorknock results in a listing right off the bat.

A doorknocker's first questions should be about the neighbors. Are there any properties for sale without signs, or has the owner heard of anyone contemplating a move?

When you have covered the neighbors, *then* you question the owner about the house.

If you find yourself a new agent trapped into giving an opinion of value, don't worry. Just logically say you never make a snap decision on such an important thing, and ask if it would be okay to bring one or two fellow agents through the house to establish a fair opinion. You can also check recent comparable sales on the street.

But before you go running back to the office to ask your manager or a couple of busy agents for their time, ask the owner why he or she wants to sell. If there appears to be no reason for selling, you can assume it is simply curiosity, so you back off gracefully but leave the door open.

Every Caller on Your Advertising
Where do you think the people move from who are looking for a house? From another dwelling of course.

When you have just about ended the conversation regarding your own listing, and it hasn't resulted in an appointment to show the property, start probing about the caller's own residence. If it is owned by the caller, a potential listing is on the other end of the line.

This also applies to commercial, industrial and investment properties. Perhaps the caller has something to sell.

Never end ad calls without asking if you can help the callers move some of *their* property.

Personal Recommendations
Don't be afraid to let your friends and acquaintances know you are in business. And don't be afraid to *ask* for their business.

A wealthy industrialist, after signing a large insurance contract, was asked by a friend why he didn't give *him* the business. "You never asked me," said the industrialist.

You aren't going to hurt anybody's feelings by asking for their business.

After you have sold a property to (or for) a happy client, ask for his help and advice in obtaining some more business.

How many business cards do you hand out in a day? How many times have you socialized with people without letting them know you are in the real estate business? Plenty, I'll bet.

The squeaky wheel gets the grease!

Past Business Acquaintances

Make a list of everybody you have done business with in the past, regardless of their occupations.

Send them all a friendly greeting telling them you are now in the real estate business, expressing your desire to help them whenever possible.

One week after the mailing, telephone them to say hello and ask if they received the mailing.

Ask them all to place your name and phone number in their address book.

Contacts From Business and Social Clubs

In the atmosphere of a club, members don't like pushy reminders about a fellow-member's occupation.

Be subtle about it. But make sure as many as possible know you are in business.

A good opportunity to remind them *all* is at Christmas time when you can mail each one your business calendar for the coming year.

Much business is generated in clubs. Quietly. You can get a piece of the action by playing your cards right.

Telephone Solicitation

Tough slugging, but a great way to practise your salesmanship to a stranger over a telephone.

Take a long list of names and telephone numbers from a street directory of your territory, and call ten from the list each day.

Introduce yourself. Be yourself. Heard of any new listings in the area ma'am? Like to keep in touch and know what's going on in *my* area.

Once in a while you will find a yacky neighbor who will really fill you in!

It can and does produce business, but don't overdo it or you'll go stale and get that tired old feeling.

Neighbors

What do you say when you discover a house on your own street is listed with another agent?

Your first reaction may be that "Oh well, the agent is probably a personal friend of the owner."

Not necessarily so. The truth is that you just might have obtained the listing if the neighbor knew you were in the real estate business.

How many homeowners on *your* street know you are in business?

And if they don't, why? Get cracking.

Merchants Who Get Your Business

We all have our favorite merchants. Dry cleaners, cigar stores, drug stores, gas stations, etc. How many of them know you are in business?

When you patronize a shop, remind the clerk or owner with your business card that you will be pleased to hear of any possible real estate action of *any kind*.

When you get to know the merchants on a long-standing basis, it is quite possible that they will keep some of your cards. Merchants *do* hear of neighborhood moves, and they *do* have strangers walking in once in a while, asking questions about local real estate in their casual conversation.

Lawyers

Many lawyers have their own favorite real estate agents, but remember that lawyers also work on a "two-way street."

We all know some lawyers, and we have steered business their way. Don't be afraid to ask for their recommendation to clients.

Also, whenever you are in lawyers' offices, ask them if they have any private mortgage money. They, and it, can be a good source of funds for that second mortgage you need to make the deal.

Lawyers handle estates. Estates have real estate to dispose of. Agents sell it.

Out of Town Owners

The next time you are in an assessment office, take an hour to go through the rolls looking for absentee owners. Especially property owners who live out of town.

Write them a letter offering your services. Once in a while you will hit an owner at the right time, and bingo, you have a listing.

Advertising for Special Properties to Sell

Don't place an advertisement saying you are "looking for 3 or 4 bedroom bungalow in Goose Heights for a buyer." Be more specific.

Ensure you do have the buyer looking for what you are seeking in the ad, and show the ad to the buyer; let him know you are working hard on his behalf. It won't stop him calling other agents, but it will slow him down. Anyhow, the ad just might get you a listing if your buyer won't buy it.

Neglected Properties

Whenever you see a run-down old clinker, knock on the door and tell the owner you are looking for building lots. It's understandable.

But make sure the person answering the door *is* the owner. A tenant may not like the idea of moving. If it is not the owner, make a note of the address and check it the next time you are in the assessment office.

Industrial Personnel Officers

Whenever you have a house listed in an industrial area, ensure that the personnel managers of local industries are made aware of it. Who knows, there may be a new employee in a plant waiting to buy the house from you.

It also gives you an opportunity to let the personnel manager know you are active in the area. It could lead to business from employees coming *or* going.

Miscellaneous
Scan this list. You will probably think of someone here who can help you.

Architects	Banks
Designers	Trust companies
Interior decorators	Mortgage lenders
Barbers	Accountants
Milkmen	Ministers, etc.
Routemen	Insurance agents
Postmen	Business transfer notices
Doctors	Legal notices
Dentists	

4

Private Sales Can Work for You

Here is some advice I have given buyers about those private For Sale signs.

Keep it in the back of your head. Someday you may get a deal out of it.

Does a private For Sale sign on a house mean you can save some money?

Maybe. Maybe. But before rushing down to the bank to get your check stiffened, maybe I can save you some more.

The basic reason for selling privately is quite obvious. To save money. Specifically—the real estate agent's fee. The vendor will probably point this out to a buyer, observing that since no one is going to pay an agent, there will be a great saving for the buyer.

This can be dynamite to an unsuspecting buyer's pocketbook, especially if he thinks he too is being clever in avoiding a real estate agent.

There is certainly nothing illegal or wrong in selling one's own property privately, but if you are considering such a move, ensure that it is done properly.

The most vulnerable buyer is one who is searching for a house in an unfamiliar area. Values are not consistent from province to province, city to city, and not even within the confines of one city or town.

A standard six-room bungalow in an urban fringe town with a market value of $75,000 could very well command as much as $175,000 in the city and, not only that, the city property would probably be on a smaller lot.

A buyer, after searching in the city and becoming discouraged with its inflated market, could reasonably look to the suburbs and surrounding towns. Coming across a private sign in a town on a comparable $175,000 city property could be an expensive experience. If he found the vendor asking $100,000 for the property, it might seem like a bargain, when in reality the local market price might dictate a value of $25,000 less.

I am not suggesting that a buyer should ignore a private sign, because the home might be very suitable for his particular needs. What I do strongly suggest is that a true and reasonable local value be determined.

This can be done by employing an established local real estate broker to do one of the following:

- Appraise the property. A verbal opinion would probably cost about $75. A written one perhaps $200.
- Act as a counsellor for the purchase, for a prescribed fee.

A vendor who is not actively engaged in real estate is not really qualified to appraise his own home, the basic reason being that he has a built-in inflated idea of what his own property is worth.

As a matter of fact, real estate brokers often enlist the aid of other brokers in valuing their own homes.

So an appraisal must be done to establish just what the market value is. If the private seller is doing a good job, he will have had an appraisal done to justify the selling price, but this should be confirmed independently.

The purchaser, in objecting to paying for an appraisal, is not being realistic, and if the seller is uncooperative about having one done, there may be a fly in the financial ointment.

The appraisal will only come into the picture when a purchaser has found a property he is genuinely interested in buying, and when one reaches this stage, it is better to be out a modest sum rather than thousands, which could happen. If the appraisal should justify the private seller's price, then it would certainly be worth the appraisal fee to know that at least one did not pay more than the reasonable market value of the property.

Retaining a broker on a fee basis means the broker would have to represent the buyer in negotiating the purchase, and this would cost much more than an appraisal. If one did not wish a broker to go this far, at least the broker could draw up a proper offer, possibly with advice that could save the buyer money.

Or, have your lawyer draw up the offer, but have it strictly understood that you are paying for legal advice and not for the negotiation of the purchase. There could be a big difference in fees here.

Like I always say, if you like it, want it and can afford it, buy it. But do it right.

5

The New Listing

A common question buyers ask is "how old is the house?" Now, be honest with yourself. Look at your own listings—can you answer this simple and logical question about them all?

Look at the Real Estate Board M.L.S. listings. How many mention the age of the house? Why not? Obviously because the listing agent didn't bother. If it is on the listing, the Board will publish it, so do your fellow agents and yourself a favor and list the age of the building.

"How's the roof?" is another common question. Is your usual reply "it seems to be okay"? Such laziness. The vendor will tell you about the roof, so ask him—and know. And put it on the listing.

In addition to the usual information, here are some reminders for your next listing:

- The age of the building
- The condition of the roof and the remaining life of its guarantee
- The age of the furnace and its condition, including the name of the serviceman familiar with it
- Wiring: How much is copper? How old is it? What are its services?
- Plumbing: Copper? Plastic? What?
- The flooring under the carpeting: Hardwood, softwood or plywood?
- Is the house insulated?
- Schools—secondary, public and separate
- Nearest public transportation
- Exact mortgage details, including the name of the mortgagees
- Verify the taxes at the municipal offices

Make a note of all these points. When you use them in addition to all your other information, your buyers will think you are one smart cookie.

As soon as your new listing is typed on your office form, here are some suggestions that will save you a lot of time and not a few headaches in servicing it.

You must have the listing information *on your person* and *on your desk* at all times. In addition to this, you must have street and area information relating to the listing in the same place.

So, photocopy the listing *and* a page from your pocket street directory (or your own drawn map) on an 8½ x 14 sheet of paper. Together on the same page. One for your pocket or purse and one for your desk. It is important to have it on your person because you can receive a call anywhere, and your desk is a long way away.

Circle the location on the map part of the sheet in red. Now what have you got?

You have a sheet of paper not only with the listing information, but with the area map. All together. When you receive calls on the listing, you can talk all you want, with confidence, because of your ready reference.

The map part is important, because you can talk location much better than you ever could by memory, no matter how long you have serviced the area.

This same system can be used on *all* the listings you are working on. When you are showing properties to potential buyers, you can go from one showing to the next with precision, because you will have the maps and the listings together. It will save you a lot of time, believe me.

If you have an open house for agents and find that forty or fifty have turned up to inspect the property, for God's sake don't leave the inspecting agents' cards with the vendor. If the listing doesn't sell during your agreement period, the vendor would probably go through the agents' cards and list the property with someone else——especially if another broker had about a dozen of his agents through the property.

Of course this wouldn't happen if you service the vendor properly, now would it? And how do we service vendors?

The most basic way to keep a listing and keep the vendor happy is to *keep in touch with the vendor*. Boy, do they get annoyed when they list property and never hear from their agent for days and days and days. And so they should.

Even bad news is often better than no news. Vendors are only interested in their own property. They are anxiously awaiting a satisfactory sale, and every day this is on their mind. *Never* ignore a vendor for long periods of time. Keep in touch every couple of days. Set aside a period of time each working day for the specific purpose of calling your vendors.

When their house is shown, they want to know what the potential buyer thought of it. Tell them.

Vendors are going to pay you thousands of dollars for moving their property, and they are certainly entitled to hear from you with reasonable consistency. If you don't keep in touch, you'll probably lose the listing.

6

Listing Office Space

There is a lot more to listing office space than a few brief details. Consider the following checklist, which was kindly provided by the late John B. Hudson, F.R.I., F.R.I.C.S.

Check the Location
1. Public transportation (buses, subways, GO train, airport)
2. Accessibility to expressway, parkway and freeway
3. Traffic congestion at rush hours
4. Parking
5. Restaurants, hotel and convention facilities
6. Banks, post offices, shopping
7. Type of neighborhood: improving, stable or deteriorating
8. Location of residences of present staff and potential employees
9. Accessibility for clients, customers and suppliers

Check the Space
1. Age, quality and image of building
2. Ownership and reputation of management (are existing tenants satisfied?)
3. Roster of present tenants
4. How long has space been vacant? Is other space vacant? Why?
5. Number and size of floors, number of tenants (with eye to future expansion, theirs and yours)
6. What is the rental rate per sq. ft.? Is the given floor area accurate? What is the basis used for measurement? Does the measurement include a percentage of common area?
7. Think in terms of cost per month or per annum (an efficient floor layout may well bring a better building within your budget)

8. Check the width of the window module and the perimeter induction units and the size and spacing of the columns
9. Where the terms Gross and Net are used, determine exactly what these mean in each case as they relate to (a) floor area (b) services included
10. Allow 150 to 200 sq. ft. per person depending on "Chief to Indian" ratio
11. Are the following included, and, if so, are they satisfactory? heat, water, air conditioning, janitor service, window cleaning inside and out, snow removal, landscaping, fluorescent lighting (check candle power), washrooms, drinking fountains, elevators, windows (double or single glazed?), window coverings (drapes or blinds?), wiring, soundproofing, floor loading, underfloor ducts, services in ceiling, staff coffee and eating facilities
12. Type of heating and air conditioning system—does the lessor pay for its maintenance and hydro costs? Will air circulation be effective when partitions are erected?
13. Is there a partition or leasehold improvement allowance? Does the lessor insist on a particular type of partitioning?
14. Who pays for—
    • demolition of existing partitions
    • floor tiling, repairs or renewal: does lessee receive a tile credit or a broadloom allowance if he broadlooms instead?
    • interior painting of ceiling and walls—does this include interior partitioning?
    • changes to air conditioning duct work and lighting
    • power and telephone outlets
    • hydro charges, fluorescent tube replacements, ballasts and starters
15. In offices previously occupied, specify all items to remain for your use, e.g. partitions, counters, shelving, broadloom, drapes or blinds, window air conditioning units
16. Parking—how many spaces and are they reserved? Are they a part of the lease, or can the present monthly

cost be increased? Is there additional parking in the area?

17. What is the most desirable lease term? Will a longer lease protect against future rent increase or expansion by a larger tenant? Is this type of space in demand so that, if necessary, it could readily be sublet? Has the tenant the right to sublet? Can the tenant keep any profit rental obtained in so doing?

18. If a long lease, will the lessor repaint at his cost at say five year intervals?

19. Is there an option to renew? If so, at what rental? Is the space under option to another tenant at a later date?

20. Can the lessee be given notice to vacate if the building is sold or demolished? If so, is there any compensation for tenant's improvements?

21. Check if lessee is required to restore premises to their original state on termination of lease or if improvements are to remain and become lessor's property

22. Has the lease a realty tax escalator clause, an escalator clause for operating expenses, or both? What is the base year for each? In new buildings, check how the base year relates to extent of completion and percentage of occupancy — the later the base year the greater the advantage to the tenant

23. Date of possession — check this with the telephone company, contractors, movers, furniture suppliers and allow for delays; give notice to present landlord; make sure tenant has the right of prior entry rent free to prepare the new premises for his use

24. What are the provisions for signs or identification?

25. What is the position regarding shipping and deliveries? Note if there are charges for use of elevators for furniture, materials or delivery of parcels

26. Check availability and cost of storage space

27. How is the security? Is there twenty-four-hour access? What time are the doors locked? At what hours or seasons are heat, air conditioning, elevator service curtailed?

28. Note if the landlord levies a fee for the supervision of the installation of tenant's leasehold improvements

7

Vendor Take Back Listings

Listings indicating that the vendors will be the mortgagees, first or second, should receive special note in your
listing reference files. This applies to them all, your own
firm's and M.L.S. listings.

Mark these listings with a single red X to indicate a first
mortgage, and a double XX to indicate secondary available financing.

One of the interesting aspects of mortgaging is that a
buyer with a very shaky credit rating can sometimes get
instant approval of a large loan simply by purchasing a
piece of real estate where the vendor holds the mortgage.
There is no application, very seldom a credit check, instant approval of the loan, at a reasonable rate. The
purchase mortgage feature should certainly merit more
than passing interest in the property.

The same person, of course, may get the same deal by
purchasing property with an existing mortgage, but if the
cash-to-mortgage is too steep, again he can often look to
the vendor for a loan.

Making it easy for the purchaser to buy is a cardinal
rule in selling. The more obstacles we remove, the faster
the run, and we have all seen some very fast runs in V.T.B.
deals.

When listing with this financing, be specific about what
the vendor will hold——the principal amount, the interest
rate, repayment and terms——and privileges. Put it all
down on the listing. Don't just say "V.T.B. at current
rate"——it doesn't help the selling salesman much except
to say that the buyer may get what he asks for and maybe
he won't. And worse than this is to say that the vendor
"may consider" holding a mortgage. Agents have enough
trouble with the price and other terms without running
this course also.

When listing, if the vendor is reluctant to hold a large
first, perhaps he may be persuaded to hold a smaller first

and a second. There are distinct advantages in this which you can point out to the vendor:

Two mortgage deeds means two separate securities. It can create flexibility for the lender. He could borrow against one, and then the other, without having one loan tying up all his mortgage security.

He could sell one at any time, and still have a mortgage investment.

He could make the term in the first for say five years, and a shorter term of two or three in the second.

He could get current rate interest on the first, and a bit more on the second to sweeten the pot. And remind him that both mortgage payments can be made with one check.

An agreement with a ten day condition for arranging a mortgage can go sour. We not only have to hustle around with the buyer and his mortgage application, but we have to bite our nails for a few days hoping he can pass the scrutiny of the mortgage lender's credit check.

V.T.B. means instant mortgaging, which means an instant deal with no waiting.

Do yourself a favor and work more consistently on the listings where the vendor is the lender. Don't be surprised if you get a couple of extra deals a year out of it.

8

Your Annual Sales Goal

What a business we're in. Why, all agents have to do is list and move one $150,000 property a month and their piece of the action will be about $50,000 a year each. That's executive money! The movers and shakers downtown with that kind of income have pretty fancy offices with their names on the door.

Looks good on paper, but the problem with many agents is that they are not very persistent. They will get a good commission check and then coast. And if they coast too long, the next deal doesn't come along for about three months, and the annual income isn't what it should be.

Then there are holidays. Everybody should take holidays. Some like the whole summer off. Or the whole winter. (I think some take the whole year.)

Assuming you are willing to give it maximum effort, there is no reason why you can't afford some of those nice holidays, too. But figuring your time off for holidays cuts into the annual take, so we can't really figure a twelve month year for income. Figure on about ten. That'll take care of holiday and slack time.

So now the $150,000 deal a month just brings us about $40,000. We have to work a little more.

Study chapter 29, Advertising. The high period of sales is the time to work like hell and make it. Don't take your holidays in the high period of sales. That's when you *work*.

Plan your holidays for the year at the beginning of the year and take them. Ensure that you will have the money for the holiday by *working* during the productive periods. Commit yourself and your family to the holidays—that will give you more incentive to reach your goal.

My family and I go on holidays three times a year. Ten days at a time. And we are ready financially: there are no pressing bills when we return because they are paid before we go. I can think of nothing more frustrating than buying a holiday and paying for it over a period of about two years after it is over. Put your holiday on your friendly department store account—sure, at 28 per cent a year for a couple of years when the fun's all gone. No thanks. Avoid this if you can.

So you have goals. How much do you need and want for the year? You must determine this before the year starts and then make damn sure you make it.

Prepare a chart similar to the one here for yourself. Use your own figures. Draw your goal line from day one to the end of the year in bold red ink, and then as you progress draw a black line month by month as you go. Make the chart big and stick it on your wall at home in the rec room or laundry room or on the door of the fridge in the kitchen. Somewhere conspicuous so that it will be staring at you and daring you to put your money where your chart is. And if you get ahead of the red line, don't slow down. When you go on your holidays you might be able to go first class.

The Real Estate Agent's Personal Goal and Record
1. Set the goal
2. Draw a straight line from the bottom of January to your goal by December in red
3. Keep your monthly track record up to date

One Listing and One Sale Each Month
Will Produce Wonders

	Jan.	Feb.	Mar.	Apr.	May	June	July	Aug.	Sept.	Oct.	Nov.	Dec.
$60,000												
$58,000												
$56,000												
$54,000												
$52,000												
$50,000												
$48,000												
$46,000												
$44,000												
$42,000												
$40,000												
$38,000												
$36,000												
$34,000												
$32,000												
$30,000												
$28,000												
$26,000												
$24,000												
$22,000												
$20,000												
$18,000												
$16,000												
$14,000												
$12,000												
$10,000												
$ 8,000												
$ 6,000												
$ 4,000												
$ 2,000												

9

Five Big Steps to Sales

The Big ONE

Your own listing. That's the big ONE.

Real success in real estate selling is working from the inside out. When you are working on another agent's listings, the other agent is close to the vendor (or should be), and you are handicapped.

You have no inside knowledge of how close you will be with an offer, and when it is presented you are the outsider. The listing agent knows the vendor, and after working with the vendor for some time it can be readily understood how this relationship can affect the drafting and presentation of an offer. The agent selling his own listing makes more money, and he will naturally do his best to sell it himself.

Do your best to get your own. Review chapter 3, Getting the Listing, and concentrate on the area of listing property that most appeals to you.

One of the problems in this business is that although we put our best foot forward in an earnest attempt to act in a professional manner, a large segment of society seems reluctant to allow us to do so.

We can all cite examples of giving vendors verbal appraisals with a view to listing, only to have the vendors list with the agent providing the highest price.

With many years' experience, time and time again this has happened to me. In all good conscience I would place a figure on property that I considered to be a fair and marketable one, only to be shot down in flames by someone else who came along with another $10,000 or so in mind.

The $10,000 broker would get the listing, bring it down later to something that approached my figure, and eventually the property would be sold. What's the point in providing a vendor with a reasonable assessment of value if the figure is going to be "outbid" by someone else?

It appears that this is what the public wants. It doesn't want to hear a hard, sensible approach to value. It wants to hear more. If it's pie-in-the-sky, we can always come down, and who knows, maybe, just maybe an angel will come along and pay the wish-price. Is that it?

So what do we do? Go on losing listings because we are being professional in our pricing?

If the consumer wants us to "up the price" to see what will happen, perhaps that's what we'll have to do. But when doing this, ensure that the vendor knows what the *real* opinion of value is, so that when offers do come in, you can remind him that although the sunshine price was tried, it didn't work. At least the vendor may feel that he got a fair run for his money.

If this increases the cost of housing in Canada, don't blame the agent. If the public doesn't want to *hear* the truth, *prove* it. Perhaps the only way to do that is to list high and bring them down to earth later.

But remember, a property listed at the right price is half sold the day it is listed. If your vendor won't go along with proper pricing, then you will just have to go along with it and bring him down later.

Get the listing. Eliminate the competition.

The Big TWO
You and your vendor. That's who!

Why list a property for sale if you are going to ignore the vendor? How many of you have listed a property hoping someone else will sell it?

It is not difficult to establish good rapport with your vendor. The basic ingredients for this are (1) honesty, (2) work and (3) keeping the vendor well informed.

When you list a property, don't promise the vendor something you can't deliver. If you say you will advertise the property three times a week, you must advertise it three times a week. Don't tell a vendor you'll get him $150,000 cash — the only way you can warrant this is to buy it yourself. Play it straight from square one. Here are some guidelines in creating the needed rapport between an agent and vendor:

1. After you have turned in the listing, and if possible placed your For Sale sign on the property, make it your business to get as many as possible of your fellow agents in your office to inspect the property. And ensure they leave business cards. A dozen cards from individuals will start off your relationship with the vendor on the right foot. He will know you are working for him.

   If the property is listed on M.L.S. ensure you have a notice on the listing for an open house for agents. This should be during the morning. Agents who plan their day properly inspect listings in the morning.

2. When you have prepared your advertising for the property, telephone the vendor and ask him to watch for the ad.

3. After showing the property to potential buyers who didn't make an offer, telephone the vendor and let him know of the reactions to the showings.

4. Keep in constant touch with the vendor. Nothing annoys a vendor more than to have to telephone the agent to see what's going on. The vendor should never have to make such a call.

5. If the sign, advertising and other agents have not produced concrete results within two weeks, it is logical to have another look at the price. How could an agent knock the listing price down if he has been ignoring the vendor?

   Rapport will pave the way.

6. When the price has been reduced, renew the advertising vigorously. The vendor has cooperated by reducing the price, so you cooperate by putting more effort into it.

After establishing rapport with your vendor, you will be received as a friend when the time comes to present an offer. If an agent receives hostile treatment from his vendor at this time because the vendor was ignored, the agent deserves it.

Do yourself and the vendor a favor. Keep in touch. Watch that *rapport*.

The Big THREE

You have listed a property. Good. Good. Now this is what you do.

Inspect and familiarize yourself with two comparable listings in the immediate area. They don't have to be listings from your own office of course, other brokers' will do.

Never show *one* property to a prospective house buyer. Always make appointments to show *three*. Work in threes. You must have comparisons and some basis on which to ask for an offer.

If you show just one property, what do you do then? Tell your buyer you'll see what else you can find for him? You will waste your time and the time of your employer.

Every day, familiarize yourself with other existing (and especially new) listings in the neighborhood of your listing. Check recent sales. Hammer the area—and the first thing you know, you will be the local expert.

The Big FOUR

Here are four solid sales techniques to remember:
1. When a buyer calls on an advertisement, and you are making arrangements to show property ask the buyer to meet you IN YOUR OFFICE. Then you drive the buyer to the showings, and of course back to the office. This will give you extra time with the buyer, which is most important.

   Some agents suggest that buyers meet the agent "at the property." This lazy attitude can cost an agent a sale. The agent shows a property, the buyer leaves in his own car to the next property, etc. Keep the buyer with YOU.
2. What route do you take when driving to the office? Same one each day? Take a detour. A different route every day if possible. By doing this you'll see new signs and new construction, and you will know more, learn more, and sell more.
3. If you live and work in an urban area, carve out twenty municipal blocks that appeal to your type of selling. Over a period of time most of the homeowners in the area will know who you are, you'll be the

local expert in the area and you will generate a lot of business.

Make the area your personal stomping grounds.

4. Settle on a price structure in housing that will be most comfortable for you and your personality, and stick to it.

If you are Mr. Average, you will probably feel more comfortable doing business with other Mr. Averages because you will have more in common. If you have been used to an expensive lifestyle, living in expensive homes and associating with "executives," that's your bag. You probably wouldn't feel comfortable trying to get a deal with Mr. Average.

However, if you have a flexible personality, study the sales records of your real estate board, and sell in the area and bracket of the highest volume of sales, where most of the action is. Use this as your basic area of selling for the bread and butter, and break into higher areas for the dessert.

Remember, expensive properties are shown every day, and it is in this bracket that the personality and rapport of the agent can be just the thing to tip the showing into a sale.

Be comfortable in selling. Get the message?

The Big FIVE

A sales manager who is on the ball will have a sales meeting once a week. The meeting is informal and brings everyone up to date on new listings, price changes, educational points of interest, new board and provincial regulations, etc.

At each meeting each agent will be provided with a list of current listings, and it is from this list that one can obtain a very hot source of income.

During the week previous to each meeting, the sales manager should ensure that he or she is well informed about properties that *absolutely must be sold*. The reasons are many and varied, but the one anxious tremor on the part of the vendor is that he *wants* to get it *sold*.

The FBI has its "ten most wanted" list. You get your five most wanted list. The five properties where a deal is most wanted. *The Big Five.*

Assault the list. Work on it. Advertise. Push. Push. Push. Don't be afraid of an offer. Remember the old maxim of selling—sell what *has* to be sold.

The easiest sales you will ever make will be the ones where the vendor is anxiously waiting for you to present him with an offer. He *wants* to see you.

Let the other agents work on the overpriced listings. Let *them* get slapped down by vendors who think they are being abused by offers that don't suit them. You work the big five.

Update the big five every week. You'll have to because if you hammer away at the list you'll be working on a big four or a big three before the end of the week.

Take an old pro's advice. Go get 'em. The soft ones.

Pay Attention: When a deal closes, what do you do? Grab your paycheck and run?

Slow down for a minute. You are not selling magazines. You are selling something that produces *big commissions*.

Remember tomorrow! A couple of days after your buyer has moved in, send flowers or a potted plant to the new homeowners with your best wishes. Or, better still, deliver them yourself.

Every Christmas, ensure your buyer gets your calendar and/or Christmas card.

And keep in touch. Drop in for a cup of coffee about once every six months. *Then*—don't be surprised if you get the listing when your buyer is ready to move on, plus all the business your buyer/friend has steered your way in the meantime.

10

The Agent's Seven Commandments

The first thing an agent must do after getting the listing agreement signed is give a copy to each person who signed it.

It is not good enough to provide one copy for Mr. and Mrs. Jones if Mr. and Mrs. Jones signed the listing. Each must get one. This is required by law, and if this is not done, the agent could very well jeopardize his commission for the simple reason that each co-owner signing a listing agreement would assume liability for paying the commission. So each should certainly get a copy.

According to the second commandment, the broker must give the owner an honest effort in brokerage and promote and protect the principal's interest by proper guidance in matters of price, law (with limited application) and shall render conscientious service.

In the matter of price, when presenting an offer lower than the listed price, valid, comparable, and market reasons should be given to enable the vendor to arrive at a sensible decision.

A broker is not a lawyer and therefore cannot give any legal advice, but can advise on matters in which he has been trained.

For example, when a broker presents a seller with an offer to purchase a property, the seller will not have a lawyer sitting beside him or her at the kitchen table. So he will certainly protect the vendor in important matters, such as correctly limiting the time allowed the purchaser to consider acceptance of any counter-offer.

This is a most important example, because if the purchaser gave the vendor forty-eight hours to consider the offer, and the vendor accepted it subject to some changes, the vendor should have his own time limit for acceptance by the purchaser.

Why? Because if this is not done, it may be interpreted as giving the purchaser until the date of closing in the offer to make up his mind about the counter-offer, which could be a long way down the road.

The third commandment: The broker is to offer the property at one price, and one price only. The listed price.

If an agent says, "It's listed at $120,000, but I'm sure we can shave quite a bit off that," he is certainly not thinking as much of the buyer's pocket as his own. I have known of vendors asking a friend to make pointed enquiries about price, sometimes placing the agent in quicksand.

This duty means what it says. If a prospect wants to make a lower offer, that's his business, but the agent certainly owes it to the vendor to get him as close to the listed price as possible. After all, the agent is being paid by the vendor, not by the buyer.

Under the fourth commandment, the broker will accept the agreed listing commission from his principal. This means that if the agent is fortunate enough to get a juicy deal for the vendor, and it does happen, he must not look for any bonus for being a hot shot.

Commandment five says that the broker will inform the vendor of any and all offers to purchase the property.

This does not restrict the agent to presenting signed offers. If a prospect says he would be interested in making an offer which the agent considers to be unacceptable, the agent should at least pass this along verbally to the vendor.

The vendor must be fully informed of *everything* concerning any interest in buying his property.

The broker must declare any personal interest in the transaction according to the sixth commandment.

For example, if a pal of the broker is buying the property with the agent as his silent partner, hoping to turn it over at a profit, the agent had better reveal this. Woe to the agent who gets caught.

And the seventh: The broker shall be honest, loyal to his principal and shall not be negligent.

Amen.

11

Conditioning the Vendor

There is a lot of truth in the expression "a property listed at the right price is half sold the day it is listed."

So we list a property and are sure that the price is right. But that should be just the beginning—now we can put the icing on the cake by laying the groundwork for presentation of offers to the vendor.

When getting the vendor's signature on an acceptable offer, it is good business to thank the vendor and promptly leave; we want to get the purchaser's copy to him as quickly as possible.

But when listing, it is not a good idea to grab the listing and disappear. Here is where your real rapport with the vendor starts.

The most important part of our rapport will be with a clear understanding of the price. Don't ever list a property and leave the vendor with the impression that he is going to get the listed price—that must be taken care of first. Every vendor likes to see a good solid chunky price on the listing, but a review of sales will surely show that most are overpriced.

Tell the vendor quite frankly what you think he could reasonably expect to realize for the property. You and he will know that the listing price is something to shoot at, but it is often a target. One that will allow the purchaser to negotiate. The vendor knows he will get offers, so condition him about the kind of offers he will get. He will respect you for being frank with him about it.

If he has some weird idea of price in mind, of course, walk away from the listing. Let somebody else have that headache for a couple of months.

In our anxiety to get a listing, we are prone to set an agreed price and accept it as a fact that the sale will be "cash to mortgage." Find out why the vendor is selling and also find out if he really does need all that cash. If he doesn't, go after a little help from him in financing the sale. Quite often a small three-year second mortgage can do wonders for a sale, but put the seed in the vendor's mind from the beginning.

Even if he turns the idea down, when you come in later with an offer with a second mortgage in it he will remember your mentioning it. And of course, if he won't hold it, you can always sell it for him. It is a good idea to have an offer to buy his second mortgage in your pocket. If he won't hold it, whip out the offer; otherwise forget it.

So the first two points in conditioning the vendor are price, and terms.

How about chattels? Again we tend to skip over them, and if the stove and fridge aren't going, why not be clear about what happens to them. Sometimes a vendor "might" take them with him, but more often, if he is moving up to a better house, he would really prefer to have new ones. Leaving such things up in the air by agreeing that they are "negotiable" is not a good idea. I agree that we are not in the business of selling chattels, but it has become a way of life. And for God's sake, be sure you know if the hot water tank is a rental or not. I have actually seen listings that show under "extras" the hot water tank and then, believe it or not, in brackets, "if not a rental." Imagine!

If the grounds have extensive landscaping or a hundred rose-bushes, ensure that these go on the listing. Rosebush lovers love to take their bushes with them, and this can come up in an adverse way at a later date. If the bushes don't stay, say so. And be very specific about other chattels that are not included.

What we are doing by all this is paving the way for a receptive attitude on presentation day. Presentation of an offer, that is.

Let the vendor know from square one that you may be occasionally asking for immediate, and perhaps inconvenient showings. Interruption of a favorite TV program or even a meal cannot always be avoided if we are to do a good job. Sometimes hot buyers do suddenly appear and sometimes these inconveniences happen to turn into a happy sale.

If your vendors have been counselled about all these
points, they have been conditioned by a good agent. You
will be surprised at how cooperative vendors *can* be.
Especially those who have reached good rapport with
their agent.

12

Presenting the Offer

The three most important steps in nailing the lid on a good solid deal are:
• Preparation
• Presentation
• Silence

Preparation of the offer means a lot more than simply having it typed and signed by the purchaser. This is kid stuff.

The buyer needs guidance in one particularly important area—*price*. How much? Ninety-nine-point-nine per cent of the time we work for the vendors, to make them, our principals, happy. The best way to make them happy is to get a price that will make them smile, but this, of course, is not always possible. So we, as agents, need a little quiet guidance ourselves in advising others, and here are some points to think about in considering price. Read it from the buyer's side.

In 1867 the United States government offered Russia $7,200,000 in gold for Alaska, and the deal was sealed.

Later, it was discovered that Alaska could have been purchased for *five* million, which kinda shook them up a little. Today's Russian probably winces when he thinks of the bonanza the Yankee got for his money, although at the time the Russians probably laughed all the way to the vault at this buyer who didn't know how to make an offer!

"Buy land, they're not making any more of it," said the late Will Rogers. Fine, but what about the offer? How much?

There are four basic price tags on every parcel of privately owned land in Canada.

The highest is on the land that is not for sale. Walk in cold on a man with his dream house, where he is comfortable, compatible with his neighbors, has a nice garden, is settled in the community and is supremely happy with his home and his lifestyle.

If that man's home has a current market value of
$200,000 how much would it take to get him out of there?
Certainly a lot more than $200,000. Certainly a lot more
than one would care to pay, and in isolated cases money
would *never* move him.

The next price tag down the scale is that of an owner
who is "thinking" of selling but hasn't reached the point of
making a firm decision about it.

An offer could be made to this owner. His $200,000
home might be purchased for slightly more than its market value, but if one fails with such an offer, the result will
be a free appraisal of the man's realty and inflation of his
property ego.

Now we're approaching a more reasonable situation.
The house that is for sale; on the market. (The overpriced
listings can be flushed out with a bit of viewing, so we'll
ignore them.)

How much does one offer for property on the market?

Do a little probing. Reasons for selling have a great bearing on price. Has the vendor bought another house? Is
there a breakup in the family? Is the vendor leaving town?

Which leads us to the lowest price tag of all: distress
selling. The owner has to leave town in two weeks, and he
wants his equity in cash right away. If you have the cash or
instant financing, you could obviously get a bargain.

Another bargain could be the result of a feared final
order of foreclosure or some such thing. Time is running
out, and the vendor has taken no action to force a sale of
the property which could leave him with some cash. A
final order of foreclosure is a sad thing for the owner——he
loses everything and gets nothing——unless he can find a
buyer in a hurry who will close quickly. This is what I
have often suggested to a buyer:

"Once you know the circumstances surrounding the
sale, you are ready to make an offer.

"This calls for some calculations on your part. If you
begin to bid too low, the vendor might react negatively, or
insist upon the full price.

"A higher price might be grabbed immediately, and
then you will be left wondering if you could have purchased the realty for a bit less. You'll never be sure.

"Armed with all the information you can get about the sale, and considering what you can afford, make an offer that is a little lower than what you sincerely believe to be fair under the circumstances.

"It may not be accepted, but if it is not an insulting offer, you will undoubtedly find it countersigned by the vendor with another price which you can accept, or negotiate further. And if by some chance your offer is accepted, you can smile and consider yourself a shrewd buyer.

"Of course, there are cases where you will rightfully offer a full price (or even more) for a property that you absolutely must have, but remember, an offer is the most important step in purchasing any real estate—think it out well in advance, make a realistic offer, and you probably won't be sorry."

Now, we go back to our vendors, our principals. We have to do the best we can for them, but we aren't doing our best by saying to purchasers "the price is firm, take it or leave it" or "how much to you want to offer?" The buyer has to have guidance on price. Too many deals have gone down the drain by simply waiting for the buyer to give us a figure. Some of them think they are in a flea market in Cairo and come up with figures that are so far out of line they must think we are all stupid. Guide them firmly. Let the buyer know you're there to put a happy buyer and a happy seller together, and not to act as a runner with useless offers.

Perish the thought that I would suggest such a thing, but a little birdie told me that two ploys in presenting offers that have been successful are:

- A buyer wishes to offer $150,000 for a property. To impress the vendor, an offer is drawn and nicely typed showing $155,000 as the bid; then a pen is scratched through the $155,000 and altered (and initialled) showing $150,000.

  Now the agent goes to the vendor and shows him how he did his damnedest to get the man to bid $155,000, but to no avail. He actually wanted to cut it to $148,000 but the agent worked on him for an extra half hour and got him to $150,000 says the agent.

- A buyer wishes to offer $150,000 for a property. To impress the vendor (here we go again), an offer is drawn and nicely typed showing $145,000 as the bid, then a pen is scratched through the $145,000 and altered (and initialled) showing $150,000.
Now the agent goes to the vendor and shows him how he went to work on the buyer and after an exhaustive session with him he brought him up another $5,000 from what the buyer wanted to offer. Such cheek.

Okay, so you have a figure for the offer. Now, when you have it signed and are by yourself for a few moments, *take care of the arithmetic*. Put all the figures together and add them up. You have already done this in your head or on a scratch pad, but now you formally put them down nice and neat. This is very important, because when you get to the vendor and he sees a jumbled offer with $7,000 deposit, assume a $76,000 first, pay a further $58,000 on closing, take back the balance on a second, etc., he's going to be confused. You have it all neatly laid out for him.

Price:		$165,000
Deposit:	$ 7,000	
Closing:	58,000	
First Mtge:	76,000	
Second Mtge:	24,000	$165,000

Now we are going to present it——where they separate the men from the boys, as they say.

The most direct and quickest route in the world is the one between the agent with a signed offer and the vendor. I actually heard of a man who went home to have his dinner before he took the trouble to call for a presentation, and when he got there one of his pals was walking out of the house with an accepted offer!

If you cannot find the listing agent, find his manager. Get the presentation appointment *confirmed*. If you can't find either, telephone the vendor, introduce yourself, and ask if Blank, the listing agent, is there. He probably won't be, so you say to the vendor: "I am trying to reach Blank to tell him I have an offer on your property and would like to have it presented." That's *all* you volunteer to the owner. Now the owner knows you have an offer and would certainly not entertain any others without also seeing yours.

One of the maddening things about not being able to reach a vendor is the nagging thought that an agent went in to present an offer and the sneaky bugger took the telephone off the hook. What? You never had that pulled on you?

If the offer is on another broker's listing, it is a good idea to meet the listing agent shortly *before* presenting the offer. Quite often you will find that there are obstacles you could not be aware of, and, conversely, points of presentation that could help you. We need as much ammunition as possible.

If there are two or more offers to be presented, they will naturally have to be presented in the order in which they came to the attention of the listing agent. Occasionally, one of several offers will be accepted, or signed back, but usually the agents will be asked to go back to the buyers for improvement of the offer, and an appointment will be made at that time for those who wish to come back.

Some clever agents take the buyers with them and leave them sitting in the car while the offer is being presented. If there is a sign-back, a very quick response can then be obtained and everybody can go home.

The best and simplest way to present an offer is to go in armed with a beaming, friendly attitude and then proceed in a businesslike manner. By this I mean not to let anything distract you in your presentation. Ensure you and all concerned parties are alone in a quiet room with the radio and TV turned off.

Copies of the offer will be given to everyone present, and then go through it slowly, point by point, right to the end.

The first thing a vendor will look at is the price. His eyes automatically focus on this part of the offer, and if he doesn't like it, the rest of the words won't be important to him. If the vendor drops it down immediately with disapproval, you just remind him that the buyer sincerely made the offer and the least you can all do is hear him out. Then proceed with your reading.

When you have finished, *shut up*. Don't say a word.
Now it is the vendor's turn to talk. This point of silence is
most important. The other point of silence is when you
have an offer accepted. Thank the vendor, and *leave*.

I actually had an agent present an offer on one of
my listings that was acceptable to the vendor, and before the vendor signed, which he was about to do, the
agent proceeded to tell the vendor that the flooring under
the carpet was cheap stuff, the lawn was lousy, the
backyard dirty, etc., etc. Instead of getting the signature I
then had to spend a good half hour calming the irate
vendor down after the agent had "insulted" his property.
Don't throw away a good thing because of a yappy set
of lungs.

After an indication of rejection from the vendor on
price, go through other parts of the offer for points of
approval, such as closing date, terms, etc. Narrow the
whole thing down to reach the basic objections, and then
you know what you can do about it.

When getting a sign-back, have it done with a pen of a
different kind from the original. Always use different pens
for different sets of sign-backs—it makes it easier to
know who changed and initialled what. With the sign-
back, *count* the points of initialling, and count the points
out loud with each copy as it is being initialled. This
simple method will ensure that you won't miss any.

"Meet them halfway" has created more deals in my
thirty years than any other method. If the offer is bumped
another $6,000, I'll try and come back with another $3,000.
Back and forth, always trying to slice it in half and meet
them halfway.

When you go back to the purchasers with a sign-back,
remember to go in *cheerfully*. Nothing will kill a deal
faster than a long sad face at this point. Let them know
you are getting there, doing your best to get them the
deal. If you aren't too far apart, you will get it. If you
remain cheerful.

When there is a mortgage condition in the accepted
offer for God's sake move *fast*. Would you believe that
deals have been lost on this point because the agent "took
his time"?

Confronting a property owner cold on behalf of a potential buyer can be something else. This is where a flexible personality comes in handy. The greatest in this field I ever knew was a big Irish pal of mine who could charm the birds out of a tree. Here are a couple of good examples.

We were to buy two identical plan homes for a developer. One was occupied by a beer-swilling tough guy, and the other by a gentle little old retired lady.

When the beer drinker answered the door in his underwear and loudly bellowed "Whadda you guys want?" it didn't phase my pal at all. He simply said, "We want to buy this shack of yours, kick you the hell out of here and tear it down." Whereupon the owner promptly said, "Where's the dough?" And we got it.

Being timid with a man like that results in being booted off the verandah.

The second house with the dear old lady was something else. When she answered the door the old Irish master spoke to her so gently I thought I could hear a dove cooing someplace. Yes, come in and have a cup of tea. Yes, she would really like to move, the neighborhood is not what it used to be. A trip to her lawyer's, finding the lady another nice little house, and we got that one too.

I hope you get yours.

13

Qualifying the Buyer

Someone calls on an advertisement, the agent answers a few questions, and that's it. Nothing written down, no name, phone number, nothing. Horrible isn't it? And when was the last time *you* did that?

If we were selling magazines, mistreating a telephone call or two wouldn't be too serious. The financial loss would be peanuts. But real estate? Why, a call can easily be worth $5,000 or more; we all know that. So why abuse it?

Stick a small reminder on your own telephone that reads "THIS CALL COULD BE WORTH $5,000."

Ever watch a weight lifter before he lifts the bar? He psyches himself up, which gives him more strength. You do the same. When the phone rings, take a deep breath, determine to be cheerful and pick up the phone with the five grand in mind. Treat the call with respect.

Always answer the call with a pen and paper at hand. This may sound simplistic, but we are all guilty of keeping callers hanging on the line while we "get a pencil."

Someone called *you*. Do not feel that you are imposing on the caller's time. Take your time. About 90 per cent of the calls are from people who are going to make a move sometime. Therefore, it is important to get some ammunition:

- Caller's name and telephone number
- Anything special he or she is looking for in a house?
- Family particulars
- If the call is on an advertisement, you will *know* the price range
- Is there a moving date? Moving from an apartment or house? If from the latter, you might get yourself a double deal.
- A caller who will come to the office for consultation is a *buyer*. Qualify needs—desires—wants. Be frank and honest; it will be appreciated. *Get them into the office!*

- *Never* end a conversation without asking if the caller has some real estate you could help sell.

Housing: What Is the Price Range?

Q. A buyer has $15,000 down payment. He can carry $1,000 per month. What can he afford?

A. Here is fast rule-of-thumb:

Down payment	$ 15,000
$1,000 x 100	100,000
	$115,000

The $115,000 is the approximate price range for the house.

The carrying costs will vary, of course, with the existing financing charges or new mortgaging charges, and taxes.

New Financing No. 1 (Gross Debt Service Ratio)

Q. How does one estimate the mortgage that one can carry if we know the mortgagor's gross income?

A. 1) Take 30%——27%——25% of the gross income
   2) Subtract the municipal taxes

Example:

Gross income: $30,000 x 30%	$9,000
Less annual municipal taxes	1,000
Annual mortgage principal and interest	$ 8,000

New Financing No. 2 (Gross Debt Service Ratio)

Q. How do we estimate the gross annual income required to qualify for a mortgage?

A. *Example:*

Annual mortgage interest and principal	$9,000
Annual municipal taxes	1,000
	$10,000

Ratio

$$30\% \ \frac{10,000}{30} \text{x } 100 = \$33,333$$

27% $\dfrac{10,000}{27}$ x 100 = \$37,037

25% $\dfrac{10,000}{25}$ x 100 = \$40,000

Remember——The *higher* the ratio, the *lower* the income requirements.

14

The Escape Clause

When preparing an agreement of purchase and sale that contains a condition that the purchaser is to sell his property, let us not lose sight of the fact that in the majority of cases we are agents for the *vendor*.

In the following two examples of such a condition, the capitalized letters in the second example illustrate an advantage for the vendor:

Example A
This contract may be terminated by the purchaser if, by the _____ day of _____ 19_____ , he notifies the vendor in writing that he has been unable to sell his property at _____ for completion on or before the date of completion herein. The vendor may continue to offer for sale his property, and if an offer satisfactory to the vendor is received by the _____ day of _____ 19_____ , the vendor may notify the purchaser in writing of such offer, and the purchaser shall have _____ hours from the receipt of such notice to waive his right of termination, otherwise this contract shall be null and void and the deposit shall be repaid to the purchaser.

Example B
This contract may be terminated by the purchaser if, by the _____ day of _____ 19_____ , he notifies the vendor in writing that he has been unable to sell his property at _____ for completion on or before the date of completion herein. The vendor may continue to offer for sale his property, and if an offer satisfactory to the vendor is received by the _____ day of _____ 19_____ , the vendor may notify the purchaser in writing OF THE TERMS OF SUCH OFFER, and the purchaser shall have _____ hours from the receipt of such notice TO AGREE IN

WRITING THAT THE TERMS OF HIS OFFER BE AMENDED
TO MEET THE TERMS OF THE NEW OFFER WITHOUT THE
RIGHT OF TERMINATION, otherwise this contract shall
be null and void and the deposit shall be repaid to the
purchaser.

The agent who obtained the offer from the purchaser will
do the utmost to expedite a sale of the purchaser's property to ensure himself of pay checks in two closings. He
may be prone to use Example A, because by using Example B, it would be possible for the vendor to obtain a
better offer, and one which the purchaser may not wish to
match. In such an event, the agent would lose the sale to
another agent.

However, as agents and sub-agents, we do represent the
vendor. With the foregoing in mind, which clause would
you use?

15

Land Assembly

Being the agent in assembling land can be exciting and profitable, but if one isn't careful, downright expensive.

The woods are full of "developers" who spend a good deal of their time finding agents who will swallow a big line of crap and go to work for nothing. It is just great being a good guy, *but you can't spend it.*

Assuming you are approached by someone who tells you he wants to make you a bundle by helping with his grandiose plans to develop a certain block of property, obtaining options and securing conditional offers, consider the following:

Listen to him. Hear his full story. Express keen interest. Accompany him to the site, get all the details you can of the plan, and then make an appointment to see him again in a couple of days. During the two day interval, you can do yourself a lot of good by:

- Checking the zoning and asking questions in the municipal planning department. Going over the assessment rolls is very important. If more than one property is owned by the same party, or if there are a few absentee owners, it could spell trouble with hold-outs in an assembly.
- Speaking to a few homeowners in the area and doing a little probing. Get the owners' feelings about making a move; about redeveloping the neighborhood. If you are lucky, you will meet a gabby one who will be delighted to tell you all about the neighbors. Don't worry about this advance probing hurting your chances for success, because the day you make your first presentation it will spread like the plague. This initial approach can save many headaches and time.
- Getting a credit report on the man. Find out all you can about him and his company and associates. Especially the company and its financial strength.

Armed with all this information, meet your man again and go into more detail. Find out how *you* are going to get paid.

Your man might be one who intends to tie up the area for peanuts and go for a rezoning, in which case he may intend to use your services at no cost to himself; his reasoning being that if the deals close, you will be paid by the vendors. Working on this basis should be a no-no for you.

I have developed sites for apartment buildings, commercial ventures and a giant office building. Here are some guidelines I recommend as good working arrangements between agent and purchaser.

The first consideration will be to decide just who you are going to work for, the buyer or the seller. In an assembly, it is better to work for the buyer. The buyer pays you, so he is your principal. Your client. You have just one party to look to for compensation.

Being paid by the buyer has a distinct advantage, and that is that the vendors will be more receptive to your call because you are not asking them to pay any commission. And let's face it, why should they? You are really not working for a vendor in an assembly.

Get a contract of employment. Study the following example, especially the arithmetic:

THIS AGREEMENT made in duplicate the 15th day of December 19___,

BETWEEN:

> COMFORT REALTY LTD of the Town of Karp, in the County of Halton, Real Estate Broker (hereinafter referred to as "Comfort")
>
> OF THE FIRST PART

——and—— ZOOM CORPORATION LIMITED, a company amalgamated under the laws of the Province of Ontario (hereinafter referred to as "Zoom")

> OF THE SECOND PART

WHEREAS Zoom is desirous of obtaining the forty-two (42) properties outlined in yellow on a Plan of Survey attached hereto as Schedule "A" (hereinafter referred to as the "42 properties");

AND WHEREAS Comfort has agreed to obtain Options to Purchase or Agreements of Purchase and Sale in respect of the 42 properties in accordance with this Agreement:

NOW THEREFORE in consideration of the entering into these presents, the parties mutually agree as follows:

1. Comfort agrees to faithfully attempt to obtain forty-two individual Options to Purchase or Agreements of Purchase and Sale of the 42 properties on terms and conditions agreeable to Zoom.

2. Comfort shall be entitled to One Thousand Dollars ($1,000) from Zoom for each and every Option or Agreement of Purchase and Sale which Comfort obtains which is executed by each individual Vendor and Zoom, payable on receipt by Zoom of a completely executed Option to Purchase or Agreement of Purchase and Sale.

3. Comfort shall be entitled to a further Four Thousand Dollars ($4,000) from Zoom on the successful closing of each and every agreement referred to in Paragraph 2 above.

4. In the event the aforesaid 42 properties are successfully closed for a total purchase price of not more than Ten Million Dollars ($10,000,000), then Comfort shall be entitled to a further sum of One Hundred Thousand Dollars ($100,000) from Zoom, payable on the date when the last of the said properties is successfully closed.

5. In the event the aforesaid 42 properties are successfully closed for a total purchase price of less than Ten Million Dollars ($10,000,000), then Comfort shall be entitled to a further sum equal to ten per centum (10%) of the amount by which Ten Million Dollars ($10,000,000) exceeds the actual total purchase price, payable on the date when the last of the properties is successfully closed.

6. Nothing in this Agreement shall obligate Zoom to accept any Option or Agreement of Purchase and Sale which Comfort brings to Zoom.

7. This Agreement shall be binding upon the parties hereto, their respective heirs and executors, but is not assignable.

(followed by attested signatures)

This is a good contract. It ensures that the agent receives some payment as the assembly progresses, with a lump sum on each closing. He then has two possible financial bonanzas for doing a good job. If the options are not exercised, at least he has received *something* for his time.

Many developers would rather have the agent work on "conditional offers," whereby a nominal sum is placed in trust only to be returned to the "buyer" when the deal does not close. The agent usually gets nothing for this work, being told to look to the vendor for a commission on closing.

An option is much better to work with than a conditional offer. The offer contains so many conditions that it confuses a vendor, or requires a trip to the vendor's lawyer for explanation. The option is clean, precise and gives the optionor (vendor) some cash whether it is exercised or not.

The option itself should be prepared to work in several stages:

When there is a large number of properties to be optioned, the agent and buyer should have an indication of possible success or failure of the project within a few weeks, so stage one of the option will be for a period of two months, with a nominal sum of perhaps $1,000 payable to the vendor for the two month option.

Included in this two month option will be two renewal periods, with larger sums of money involved.

If, at the end of the initial two month period, the developer can see the possibility of success, he will proceed through the first renewal (6 months), and at the end of that time, if everything looks more promising, he will proceed to exercise the second renewal. Here is the meat of the option:

The option hereby granted shall be open for acceptance by the Purchaser, up to, but not after (the date to be two months' time), hereinafter referred to as the "option period," and may be accepted by a letter delivered to the Vendor or to the aforesaid agent or left at the agent's usual place of business. In the event that such option is not accepted in manner aforesaid this agreement and everything herein contained shall be null and void and no longer binding upon any of the parties hereto and the Vendor shall be entitled to retain the said sum given as consideration for the granting of this option. In the event of and upon the acceptance of this option by the Purchaser in manner aforesaid this agreement and the letter accepting such option shall then become a binding contract of sale and purchase between the parties and the same shall be completed upon the terms herein provided for.

It is agreed by the Vendor that the Purchaser has the right to extend the option period as follows:

(a) For an additional period of six months from the (the date to be the last day of the two month period) upon payment to the Vendor the sum of $2,000, such sum to be non-returnable, but credited to the Purchaser on closing.

(b) For an additional period of twelve months from the (the date to be the last day of the six month period) upon payment to the Vendor of the sum of $4,000, such sum to be non-returnable, but credited to the Purchaser on closing. In the event the Purchaser exercises this option within the option period or any renewals thereof, then and in that event, it is hereby agreed that all monies paid by the Purchaser to the Vendor in consideration for this option and its renewal or renewals shall be credited to the Purchaser on closing.

To complete an assembly, the agent must move quickly. Whenever the author had a project that involved more than ten properties, I always invited other agents to help. The reason, of course, is obvious. The longer it

takes to wrap up an assembly, the higher the prices at the
tail end.

If you are acting for a vendor in an option, ensure that
the buyer puts up enough cash when exercising the option
to cover the commission. The exercising date in an option
is the day the buyer tells the vendor it is going to proceed
with the purchase.

Ditto with a conditional offer where there is a small
sum in trust. Have a clause in the agreement requiring the purchaser to put a further sum in trust before
closing.

The days of the One Dollar option are over!

If your man insists on conditional offers, keep the conditions brief and right to the point. A vendor can become
very disinterested in an offer with long-winded clauses of
condition. And with such offers, ensure that you will be
paid *something* when securing it. Don't put all your eggs
in the basket on closing.

If you think you have heard everything, let's see if you can
top these!

Once upon a time, in a certain large Canadian city, the
bylaws required that if anyone wished to apply for rezoning,
all the property owners within 300 feet of the proposed
development had to be advised of it by the municipality,
so that they could voice their objection or pleasure. So
what happened?

The developer obtained agreements to purchase the
properties he wished to redevelop, then obtained *options*
on everything within 300 feet. The price in the options
wasn't important — just get them.

When he applied for rezoning on his parcel, everyone
within 300 feet was notified. They thought that they were
going to be a part of it because of the options, so *nobody
objected*.

The rezoning on the parcel went through, and the
options were dropped.

A developer wanted a row of houses without any long-
winded conditions in the offer. So he inserted just one
in each.

When the owner of house No. 1 was approached, the offer contained a condition, and one only, that said the buyer had to obtain title to the house next door. The vendor agreed.

When the owner of house No. 2 was approached, his offer contained just one condition—title to house No. 3, etc., etc. Right down the row. The whole thing was therefore based on the deal the buyer could make on the last one in the row. Then everything else could close.

Simple, what?

Then there was the broker (imagine!) who heard that a highway was to be widened. So he sent agents all along the route listing everything in sight (there were a lot of small businesses there). The price in the listing didn't mean a thing because:

The listing agreement had a clause in it that said that if the property were expropriated or purchased by any government authority, the vendor was to pay the broker a commission. Such cheek. . . .

16

How Agents Get Shafted

Real estate agents spend most of their time creating wealth for others.

Most agents have a list of buyers looking for investment properties at discount prices. Just improve them a bit and sell them for a fat profit. When the agents come across such a property, their first thought is to start dialing numbers and get a fast deal.

The more ambitious plan is to not only get the buyer's business, but also to list the property later and sell it again. Ah, two deals.

Many agents are hesitant about getting involved. Government rules say disclosure must be made by agents buying and selling property. Why are they buying, what is the interest, are they going to resell and make a profit?

The reason for disclosure by agents is that they are supposed to be more knowledgeable about real estate. They might know some way to profit from a deal that others wouldn't. If an agent turns in his licence, he can wheel and deal all he wants. As long as he is acting legally as a private citizen, he can keep his cards close to the vest and make all the plays he cares to.

Years ago, when property values were more stable, there were actually agents who carried a briefcase full of blank—but signed—offers. The agent knew just what his buyer would pay for standard plan properties, and he would spend his time filling in the blanks and presenting two or three offers a day. Most of them would be rejected—but not all.

The agent did the legwork, received his modest share of commissions and the buyer ended up with the gravy. That's how speculation was done in the good old days. I venture to say that today some of those agents are wishing they had an indexed pension. Meanwhile, the buyers are trying to decide whether to go to Honolulu or Rome for their next break.

God bless all real estate agents. The active ones work about sixty hours a week and much of it at night. No nine to five hours, with the weekends off, for them; no pension, no sick leave, no steady income.

Every day of the week some real estate agent is getting shafted. For example:

- A property owner calls a couple of agents and gives them a song and dance about selling. After getting all the advice he can squeeze from them, he hammers a private For Sale sign on the lawn.
- An agent shows property to a buyer. The vendor tries to make a deal——without the agent——saying the listing expires in ten days, so let's get together. I consider this tantamount to grand theft but the vendor doesn't see it that way. He thinks he's a smart cookie.
- A builder has ten houses for the market. He lists just one of them with an agent. When the buyers come to view the listing, they naturally want to see some of the other houses, which aren't listed. So the builder sells ten houses——thanks to the agent——and pays a selling commission on just one of them. Pretty crafty, eh?
- Ditto for people who should be looking at modest homes but insist on seeing the big ones they'll never buy. I remember one "buyer" telling me she'd seen more than fifty homes and just hadn't found the right one yet. I was glad she told me before I became another one of her chauffeurs.

Oh yes, real estate agents are long-suffering people. The successful ones get involved and invest in real estate. Most don't because they can't afford to. Besides, they're so busy setting the other guy up for his old age, they forget about number one.

So listen, you thousands of agents out there, if you haven't got the wherewithal to do it yourself, get a couple of partners. Get involved. You can't live on the old age pension.

And you can quote me on that.

17

Guard Your Commission

A real estate buyer is protected by a lawyer, and so is the seller. Who protects the agent, the one who brought them together?

The acceptance clause in a commonly used agreement of purchase and sale includes reference to paying a commission to the agent:

"The undersigned accepts the above offer and agrees with the agent above named in consideration for his services in procuring the said offer, to pay him on the date above fixed for completion, a commission of _____ ."

You will note it does not say the commission will be paid *on completion* of the sale, but on the date fixed for completion.

In acting for a seller, nothing will raise the hair on the back of a lawyer's neck faster than reading this clause. He or she will immediately get the black marker out and change it to read that the commission will be paid on completion only.

The suspicion here is that the agent will attempt to collect a commission on the date fixed for completion whether the sale goes through or not.

I have often pondered over the clause and wondered why it isn't changed to simply read the way most sellers' lawyers would like to see it. No one has ever given me a satisfactory answer to the question, but I have finally figured it out.

When a buyer defaults in an agreement, the agent wouldn't have a snowball's chance in hell of collecting a commission because a buyer wasn't provided who was *ready, willing* and *able* to close. All three are necessary.

If a buyer isn't *ready* to close because he or she can't finalize financing or cash bonds soon enough to come up with some cash, it is a common practice for the seller's lawyer to "tender" on the buyer's lawyer.

This is legal notice to say the seller is ready to close and the buyer is expected to do his part. A few days are usually allowed for this to happen, and if the buyer doesn't get cracking and close, the deal may be considered dead.

The seller then puts his property on the market again, and if money is lost the second time around he may sue the first buyer for the difference. Plus the deposit money of course.

If the buyer is not *willing*, or *able* to close, it will amount to the same thing. And an agent who thinks he can claim a commission from his principal, the seller, under these circumstances is sucking wind.

Now we turn to the seller. The agent has presented the seller with a bona fide offer from a solid buyer and the seller has accepted it.

The seller has second thoughts and decides not to go through with the deal. The buyer will naturally consider the pros and cons of forcing the sale through court action, and sometimes he will figure the litigation won't be worth the time, trouble and annoyance and so forgets about it and goes on to another deal.

When this happens the seller is happy; he is off the buyer's hook. Home free. But what about the agent? Doesn't he owe him a selling commission? After all, the agent did his part by producing an acceptable offer.

Ha! The seller's clever lawyer changed that commission clause to read that a commission will only be paid on closing. The deal didn't go through, so pay him nothing.

See what I mean? The commission clause reads the way it does to give the agent a fighting chance to get what he is entitled to get.

18

Remember Number One!

How much real estate do *you* own?

If your answer is none, I am not surprised. There are probably thousands of real estate agents from coast to coast in Canada who don't own as much as one square foot of land. Why?

Well, of course, we have the lazy agent who just wants to make enough to pay the rent, keep the old flivver in running order, have three squares a day and a few beers. Many of these agents have been successful in the past, and many are prone to spend too much time talking and even bragging about the big deals they made years ago.

So, assuming you are not one of them, but one of the agents with no land holdings, what are you waiting for? Don't you believe in what you are doing for a living?

We spend a great deal of time making others wealthy, and it is pretty ridiculous to look at ourselves and realize that it is the other guy who is reaping the benefits of our years of training, expertise and know-how. So listen, get yourself a piece of the action. Even a little piece, just for openers.

You will notice that successful brokers own real estate. They certainly didn't figure on staking their future on commission and fee earnings. Follow the leaders.

About fifteen years ago I was short of cash and had a chance to get a house, a real beauty, at the right price. Did the lack of money stop me? No sir. I was *determined* to get it, and I did. I purchased it with exactly $100 down! Got a conventional first, a third party second, and secured title. The second even covered my legals. *Now get this*. The $100 equity in the house now has a fair market value of well over $200,000. And that's a fact.

Sure, I've made mistakes, too. In 1968 I moved ninety-seven acres of prime bush land just off a paved highway not far from Peterborough for $3,000. Should have bought it myself.

In 1969 I moved a 100 acre farm in a good location for $13,000 with four down. I heard that the buyer sold the barn for four grand. Should have bought it myself.

In 1972 I secured more than 150 acres on an island with a quarter mile shoreline for $9,000 with three down. I decided I didn't really need it——can you imagine that! ——and gave the closing to a friend. I heard he had later subdivided the damn parcel and reaped a real bundle. My mistake!

But brother, I don't make 'em any more. Now what do I do? Well, right now I am a hot buyer for country property. Arable land. It has to be on a concession corner.

I don't care if it is five acres or a hundred. I'll buy at market price, but only under these conditions:

- Total cash involved, no more than $5,000
- One purchase mortgage, or assume a good one
- The mortgage must carry for no more than $500 a month

So you see, the market and my own restrictions will dictate what I buy.

My mortgage payments will get cheaper and cheaper each year with our slipping dollar. Don't forget that with a constant inflation rate of just 7 per cent, today's dollar will be worth fifty cents!! (in just ten years).

Don't spend all your money on high living, fancy cars and expensive holidays.

Buy one small piece of real estate *every year*. And hang onto it. Why, in ten years' time you'll be right up there with the best of them, and when you hear some jerk bragging about the big deal he made three years ago, just smile sweetly, and be magnanimous when he bums ten bucks from you.

Be a winner. Get yourself a piece of the action. Don't end up in the poorhouse. Okay?

Part Two

THE BROKER

19

So You Want to Be a Broker?

It is the nature of things that big fish eat little fish.

Ottawa's Rideau Trust Company was swallowed by Mann and Martel, which then became United Trust, which then was swallowed by the Royal Trust Company.

Harvey Keith built a modest organization into a large organization, which was swallowed by the National Trust Company.

Mr. Gibson joined Mr. Willoughby which became Gibson-Willoughby, which was swallowed by A.E. LePage Ltd. It goes on and on, and it will never stop.

All this swallowing undoubtedly produces larger, more efficient, more productive and wealthier organizations, which in turn must surely make all the minnows wonder whether they should remain in the safety of the shallow waters, or dare to venture into the deep, dark abyss of the real estate ocean.

Many have tried, and many have failed.

It is a proud moment when a new broker stands back a few feet and, surveying the glorious effect of the first For Sale sign, realizes that at last he has finally arrived. No other listing will mean the same.

At this early stage in a brokerage career, energy is boundless. Now the broker is going to show them all!

He will be magnanimous to his former employer and cooperate on the exclusive listings, but at the same time try and persuade his former fellow agents to come swim with him.

Everything looks so rosy. The modest but attractive new office, the letterheads, the business cards, the feeling of elation that this is it. The first rung on the huge ladder of success.

Alas, six months later, all too often the picture changes. Nobody seems to be as impressed as he should be, and the new broker realizes that the current is swift with a lot of minnows competing for the bread.

His former pals don't seem to be standing in line to enlist.

Consumers aren't responding as well as they might to avail themselves of the brokerage. And the bills. Ah yes, the bills. How inexorable they are!

To you who wish to take the plunge, consider the move very, very carefully. Do not be hasty lest you suffer the embarrassment of a business failure, to say nothing of the loss of a relatively large sum of money.

Life is very relative. My late father was a clergyman; he once told me that water in hell is a dollar a drop. It took me many moons to figure that one out!

The first asset the new broker needs is money. MONEY. A financially strong broker can survive a business recession, or a loss caused by bad judgment in something attempted and not gained, but the new broker on a shoestring just cannot do it. And don't think you are any different.

A new broker must be financially able to carry the new business for one full year; not on expected revenues, but on a cash reserve.

If all the wonderful things that are supposed to happen really happen, great, but if they don't, you are not going to spend the following three or four years paying for your misfortune if you are financially sound from day one.

Socrates, the wise old bird, said "know thyself." Do you really know yourself? Do you really, honestly, believe that *you* have what it takes, and the knowledge to strike out on your own to be a successful real estate broker?

If you can honestly answer in the affirmative to the following questions, you might, you just might make it:

1. Are you in good health? Mature?
2. Have you the ability to fully determine the needs of your new venture and the capability to reach the objectives?
3. Can you direct and lead a sales force in a firm manner without causing friction?
4. Can you properly organize a new venture and truly determine its priorities?
5. Have you the strength to be honest with yourself?
6. Are you willing to work sixty hours a week?

7. Are you willing to place the interests of your organization above any one person, including yourself?
8. Can you analyze business trends to your special advantage?
9. Have you a record of cooperating with fellow agents in the past?
10. Can you stick to a decision once it has been made?
11. Is there harmony in your personal life?
12. Have you got the guts to make an unpopular decision?
13. Are you constantly improving your knowledge by supporting your real estate board meetings and seminars?
14. Has your income been more than $40,000 during each of the last three years?
15. Are you *really* ambitious? Courteous? A self-starter?
16. Last but not least...Do you dress well, drive a clean car, behave yourself and look successful?

Good luck——and don't forget the money.

20

The Sales Manager

Real estate sales managers are special. Very special. And if they are productive, they are very, very special— because they are a rare breed who are hard to find.

We all know of some brokers who appear to change their sales managers as often as they change their shirts, as the saying goes. The obvious reason is that the individual and the job just didn't go together. But there is much more to it than that.

The sales manager of a pencil maker could move to sales management with a clock maker without too much difficulty. He studies his new market, applies his know-how with the sales force and goes to work. Pencils or clocks.

But real estate? No way.

Real estate sales managers must know the real estate business well enough to direct and counsel a sales force of experienced, specially trained people on their own level. They cannot afford to sidestep a thing, and if they don't know their business inside out it will be glaringly obvious to the agents in very short order.

So we need one who not only knows the real estate business as well as, or better than, the top agents, but one who knows how to reach rapport with the staff and direct it. A rare breed indeed.

Many sales managers in real estate are recruited from within the organization. It is a logical step, because the one promoted is familiar with the company policy, its management and sales staff.

Not all agents, of course, aspire to a position in management. Too restrictive. Too demanding, and, quite often, not enough money.

The underlying and motivating factor of sales managers is profit. Profit for the company, profit for them and profit for their sales force. No profit. No job. Period.

Sales managers tackle their first office because they want to be more than just another face in the crowd. They want to accomplish something more than what they have been doing for years. It is a challenge. They believe they can do it, and sincerely want to have a crack at it.

They bring with them not only full understanding of the problems in real estate, but a sincere desire to help the agent solve the problems.

Perhaps above all, they must bring with them a large measure of character.

Good character is one of the attributes bank managers like to find in their borrowers. It is the mark of an individual, qualities they possess that set them apart from others. Something distinctive that qualifies them for certain tasks.

They must be ones who fully understand and accept the long, arduous and unreasonable hours required of them. Helping new agents present offers at all hours of the night, for example.

They must have an understanding spouse——very understanding. When sales managers were agents, they knew when they could take the night off without interruption, but not now. A salesman could call at any hour with problems.

They must place the interests of their employer above their own interests, which isn't always easy.

They must be ones who will earn and retain the respect of their salesmen, and maintain a good sense of rapport.

They must be ambitious. Boy is this important! Exercising one's ambition without stepping on too many toes calls for diplomacy.

They must be able to organize long work loads for their sales force to ensure that they, in turn, succeed.

They must be original. Someone who can pop the light bulb with bright and fresh ideas to stimulate business.

They must be friendly and firm. Make decisions and stick to them regardless of the degree of popularity.

They must also be flexible. Able to call a spade a spade when things go wrong and let somebody else do the crying over the spilled milk.

They must be able to spot winners and losers, and never be afraid to say goodbye to the losers and clean off their desks for some winners.

They must be patient with both neophytes and experienced people. Be able to encourage and direct them to greater effort and rewards.

They must be determined organizers, know how to put it all together and make it work.

They must be leaders. Not parade square sergeants, but ones who can quietly get the salesmen to carry out their directives. And follow up on them.

They must be honest with themselves. Take stock once in a while and see what they are doing right, and doing wrong.

No one can be all things to all men, but the sales managers of real estate firms with outstanding and consistent sales records sometimes appear to be just that.

What is it that makes one group of salesmen work like dynamos for one manager, and flop all over the place for another? It is a combination of the foregoing, with a lot of that good old fashioned human electricity thrown in for good measure. The invisible thing nature gives to one and denies another. As Sophie Tucker said, "a good man is hard to find"——especially a real estate sales manager.

An apparently insurmountable problem with small brokers is the necessity of having a sales manager compete with the salesmen. The small broker with a small sales force often cannot afford to pay a sales manager a living wage strictly out of an overriding commission and/or salary because the commissions just aren't there to support it.

This may create suspicion in the minds of the salesmen that the sales manager will take undue advantage of the position and grab all the goodies.

If you are faced with this, it is important that when the sales managers do turn in a listing or creates a sale, they should be quite frank about it and tell the sales staff how the business was generated.

21

Recruiting the Salesman

We don't *hire* salesmen! Hire is defined as payment for the use of a *thing*. Salesmen may be things to some brokers, but not to successful ones.

A better word is employ. We employ salesmen. To employ is to use the services of—to keep in one's service, and we certainly want to keep a good salesman in our service as long as possible.

To get the employee we must use salesmanship. Recruiting is selling. Selling a good prospective salesman on the advantages of joining one sales force over another.

Why would a new, or experienced, salesman want to join your organization? Because it has more to offer? Bigger commissions? More listings? Bigger name? Nicer offices? Closer to home? Be honest with yourself: Why would anyone prefer to work with *you*?

Recruiting is naturally tougher for the little guy who wants to expand. He cannot expect much success simply by hanging a sign in his window saying he has openings. Recruiting must be planned salesmanship. Strategy.

One of the most abused instruments in selling is the telephone. Every time it rings on a salesman's desk he should be aware of the fact that the call could be worth a couple of thousand dollars to him. With the broker recruiting salesmen, the call could be worth what—$20,000 a year, $250,000 over ten years? The recruit could do it for you, so *respect that call!*

When a call comes in response to your advertising for new salesmen, keep the conversation brief with your potential windfall. You don't want to fire your best shots sitting there talking to a voice at the other end of the line.

Tell the caller how pleased you are that he called, and let him know that you are *genuinely* interested in meeting him personally.

And for God's sake, don't be late for your appointment!

When he arrives be cheerful, pleasant, and make him feel welcome. Don't sit across a desk looking like some bank manager about to say nix to a loan. Be natural. Smile. Get him a cup of coffee. Make sure he is relaxed before you say one word about the object of the interview.

Many years ago I found myself in England applying to be an officer in the Kenya police force. For my interview I was ushered into a sparsely furnished room containing two chairs behind a small table, with one chair (for me) facing this.

I sat alone in the room for about five minutes, and then in strode two men. One grizzly old boy in civilian clothes, and a younger man in the uniform of a police officer.

They didn't say a damned word to me for a full two minutes, which of course seemed like twenty. Just stared at me. Suddenly the old boy barked, and I mean barked: "Why do you want to go to Kenya?"

Well, to tell the truth it just dawned on me at that time that I hadn't really thought about it, and I told them so. Which of course ended my trip to Kenya before it began (thank God). The Kenyan recruiting campaign undoubtedly filled its quota of required recruits, and also rejected the unrequired ones, like myself.

If you want to have most of your sales applicants beat a hasty retreat, try the Kenya method. But one of the glaring facts about sales recruiting is that it is next to impossible to tell by looking at a person if he will be a successful real estate salesman, and so we cannot afford to brush anyone off without giving the interview the old college try.

Here is something to think about. Many very successful real estate people went into the business because they saw a better life than being perhaps a grocery clerk, a bank officer or a plumber. We all know of some outstanding success stories.

If you had to select one of these two applicants, which would it be?

- A thirty-four-year-old cab driver, married, three children, four years' cab experience
- A just-retired senior executive

Your first consideration would be the potential success of the one you employ. Naturally.

The retired executive, newly on his own, will probably be a misfit for a year or two after retirement. He has no book of rules now, no one to direct him, and no one he can direct. He is, at last, all alone in the world.

He has his pension check, so he probably won't be on your back for a draw.

He may know a few people who could help him in his real estate career. But he may not be the type who is aggressive enough to go after them.

He may be searching for "something to do." He doesn't really have to work, but on the other hand he doesn't want to hang around the house all day.

He may be just your man.

The cab driver is young, aggressive (he wants to improve his lot in life).

He has a family to feed, and to do this he is obviously not afraid to work and put in the hours.

He knows the city. Every street. He could look at a listing and not only know where it is, but what the whole neighborhood looks like.

He is used to talking to people from every walk in life.

He also may be just your man.

Unless it is your intention to employ everyone who applies, you will have to establish priorities for yourself. A set of pros and cons. How will one look better than another?

Want to move farms? What better man to list them than an ex-farmer?

Large expensive estates? Find the one who moves in that circle.

Be wary of the glib agent who jumps from one firm to another.

Place a price tag on the head of every recruit. Budget. Be prepared to spend money, and lose money.

I have found that the best way to relax a potential agent on the first interview is to quietly suggest this: "Tell me about yourself."

This will give your potential breadwinner a chance to collect his thoughts and start talking. If he is at all nervous, it will cause him to relax.

Pick up some points in his conversation you can enlarge upon, such as mutual interests. Now you are reaching rapport.

Tell the recruit about yourself. Your company. Tell him how you can help *him*. Never mind you, you already know how he might help you!

Make comparisons. Illustrate the advantages of working as a team with a small (or large) broker. Stress your two-way street for agent and management.

Show him around. Introduce him to some agents.

How far you can go to help a new agent is up to you, your management and your resources. But you must have a concrete sales plan to sell the recruit on working with you.

Above all, be honest about the probability of success in this business. You might, for example, illustrate a comparison of six months' sales of your sales force (without mentioning names of course). Show what your top agents' earnings are, and *why* they are top agents. Recruits want to hear about success, how *they* can succeed.

Find out about the recruit's family and lifestyle. This is important, because whether you like it or not, you may be supporting the whole family.

There should be two interviews, the first when you size each other up, and the second when the cheese could become more binding. Unless of course you have a hot shot on your hands who is chomping at the bit and you would like to give him a desk right away.

When processing new agents, have a fast bonding service prearranged, and documentation quickly executed.

Every new agent should be provided with a briefcase containing everything that goes into a real estate briefcase, including a tape measure. Also, the new agent should be provided with a copy of your company policy. If you don't have one printed, get one. Put it down.

There should also be a copy of a company agreement signed by the broker and new agent. This would cover part of your two-way street in employment.

And remember, when you are interviewing a potential agent, hold all calls. Let the telephone ring *after* the interview.

22

The Salesman's Contract

There appears to be a tendency in small brokerage houses to operate on a palsy-walsy basis, with a verbal understanding of what the salesman will get and what he won't get.

On the part of the salesman, this can lead to confusion, ambiguity and eventually a feeling of resentment that the broker isn't the good guy he is supposed to be. This feeling can build up in an agent until he begins to tell his pals in other firms, and anyone who will listen that his boss is, confidentially, an S.O.B.

His pals, in turn, tell others, and by the time it gets back to the broker, my God, sir, he is a genuine ogre.

Most of this can be eliminated by communication between the broker and agent—in other words, person to person. And, with the exception of a born sorehead, perhaps with a chip on his shoulder, who really shouldn't be in real estate in the first place, it can be 99 per cent eliminated if the broker and salesman have an understanding right from square one *in writing*.

Every broker should surely have a company policy in writing. This is essential, and if you haven't got one, get a copy of one from a large broker and use its guidelines to fit your own needs. A basic part of it would be a clear understanding about a complete breakdown in commission and fees under *all* circumstances.

The salesman, in addition to being given a copy of the company policy, should be provided with an employment contract. This will outline in a no-nonsense manner just what the salesman and broker will expect of each other.

The basic way to establish one is to outline the points for each party you wish to have incorporated in the agreement, and then take it to your lawyer for editing and drafting for the printer. The same agreement will apply to all sales personnel.

The agreement should be in three parts: the responsibility of the company, the responsibility of the salesman, and termination agreement.

The company responsibility basically is to:

- Provide the salesman with all the operational "tools of the trade" such as signs——the ones with wooden stakes free——the expensive metal ones perhaps debited to his account until returned——office facilities (which will be outlined)——telephone (outline restrictions re long distance calls)——promotional material (be specific)——and advertising quotas (detailed).
- Pay the salesman the remuneration rightfully earned according to the company policy, and to pay it *promptly* when due. Here you will be specific about what deductions will be made, such as debits on a drawing account, long distance calls and other debts to the company.
- Keep proper up-to-date books of account, and have them available for examination by the salesman at reasonable times.

The salesman's responsibility basically is to:

- Devote his energies and talent to the betterment of himself and the company, and to honor the provisions of the company policy.
- Pay for all his own expenses, such as those for his automobile and others except those outlined in the company policy and others that may be authorized by the company from time to time (such as trips out of town on bona fide deals, and how costs will be shared).
- Agree to decisions made in arbitration by the company and to share costs of disputes on a pro rata basis.
- Agree to never bind the company to any financial commitments unless specifically authorized.
- Treat the affairs of the company in the strictest confidence and not to take undue advantage of any knowledge for personal gain.

Termination of employment will cover such points as:

- When termination can and will be effected.

- Any debt owed by the salesman to the company and vice versa, and when due and payable.
- Relinquishment of listings and rights thereto.
- Return of all company property, including keys.

These are the basics. Make your own provisions and be fair to both parties. You will both feel that you have a sounder business relationship when it is in writing.

Handshakes may be okay in life, but there are just too many things in real estate broker/salesman relationships to shake hands on.

23

The New Salesman

The neophyte's first day in a real estate office is a bit of a traumatic experience. Here he is, surrounded by "experienced professionals" who banter about their business with ease, confident about their attitudes toward fellow agents and the palaver of the real estate business. He is a bit reserved, and not only needs someone to hold his hand and introduce him to his fellow agents and make him feel welcome, but he needs immediate *direction.*

It is very important to understand that the new agent is anxious to get going in his new field, and this is where the firm and friendly hand of a *manager* is so important.

He needs the *manager's direction.*

The manager cannot afford to spend *all* day with the new agent, so here are some guidelines for his first week in his new career:

The new agent's training starts with day one, and what better way to start than to introduce him to everybody at your weekly sales manager's meeting? You do have a weekly sales manager's meeting don't you?

This will let him feel that he is getting his feet wet. He will observe, and believe me, he will pay attention to everything that is said. He will feel that he is really a part of something, and that he belongs. It is not only a good way to introduce him to his fellow agents, but he will have the opportunity to note their personalities at the meeting.

After the meeting, turn him loose with a couple of pros who are going to inspect some houses that morning. Now he is really getting into it. He can tell the family that night that here is a wide awake outfit: he not only attended the weekly meeting, but inspected some houses—and all before noon!

After lunch on day one, give him his desk, introduce him to the switchboard operator, show him his message box and then spend an hour with him.

The hour should be spent on company policy, commission breakdowns and carefully going through every item in the briefcase you supplied. Then turn him loose. Get off his back. He wants to phone the family and couple of friends to let them know where he is.

Naturally, you will have ordered his business cards beforehand!

Day Two: This is the day you are going to let him get his feet wet. Really wet. And he will enjoy every minute of it.

A sound idea for a broker's office is to have a wall map of the sales territory, with a flag pinning the location of every listing:

- White flags for open listings
- Blue flags for exclusive listings
- Red flags for M.L.S. listings.

The purpose of this is very basic. It will show the distribution and *concentration* of listings. Concentration of listings implements faster sales for new *and* experienced agents.

Direct the new agent's attention to the map. Select a listing in a concentrated area and, with the concurrence of the listing salesman, use this listing for the new agent's first newspaper advertisement.

The manager will inspect the listing with the new agent, and *two more* comparable listings in the concentrated area.

Discuss each listing thoroughly with the new agent, and *ask the new agent* to help prepare an advertisement on the one selected. Asking the agent to help is important: It enables him to feel involved, review the house and remember its good features.

Instruction about handling calls and showing the properties will be the manager's next logical step.

We have now started the new agent from the inside out. From his knowledge of the three concentrated properties, he will now be instructed to inspect other listings in the same area daily. He will become knowledgeable in the area. He will feel *confident* about *his* area. From and within this the new agent can perform wonders by *concentration* in the area.

Day Three: The new agent's first work in the morning, of course, will be to go through the new listings, and physical inspections of the ones in his concentrated area. Talk about the listings he has seen each day for a few consecutive days. Establish his pattern of listings and inspections.

Instruct him to keep copies of the listings he has inspected in a separate file.

When showing a house an agent should naturally try to show about three at one outing. Instruct the agent to copy the listing he is advertising, with a map or sketch showing its location, on a copier. Do this also to about three other listings in the concentration, the others he will be showing with the one he is advertising.

Have him keep a copy of each in his desk and a copy of each on his person. The reasons are very basic: the listings are always available for immediate reference regardless of where a telephone call is taken, and copying the location with the listing can save time in getting there without reference to a directory. Who can remember where all the streets are? I can't. Can you?

Spend an hour keeping his feet wet. Take him out for some good old fashioned cold canvassing, and have him right with you when you introduce yourselves to six home-owners. Then, let him do the talking to the next six. He will probably be as nervous as hell with the first knock, but at number six he won't feel too bad. Instruct him to do this for one hour a day for the first *month*. Such experience he will get!

If someone tries to trap him into pricing a house when he is on his own, he can easily stall by saying he never makes snap judgments on such important things, and always likes to have his manager weigh his opinion.

Day Four: Send him to the municipal office to obtain a copy of the local zoning bylaws. An agent without sound knowledge of the zoning in his area is only working at half mast. How can a real estate agent really call himself a real estate agent if he doesn't know his zoning?

Instruct the agent on its use and how it can help him in its application. (Maybe you can learn something together....)

Or better still, go to the municipal offices with him, and show him how to find ownerships, lot sizes, taxes and other useful information he will need from time to time. And don't forget to show him how to find the absentee owners he could write to for listings in his spare time.

Supply him with a few mortgage lenders' phone numbers and have him call to discuss the latest rates, funds available and types of lending they prefer. Establishing rapport with lenders is most important for the new agent.

Day Five: You have kept him pretty busy. Now sit down for an hour or so and hear what he has to say about it all.

At this meeting mutually set a financial and work goal for the next six months.

Your agent wants to succeed. You want him to succeed. Keep your door open by reminding him that one of the tools of the trade is the sales manager, and you are there to help.

With proper encouragement and direction, you could have another winner on your hands.

24

Managing the Sales Force

Forty salesmen. Ten top producers, twenty so-so producers, and ten who are going nowhere (20/50/25 per cent).

What do we do? Fire the bottom 25 per cent, improve the 50 per cent and do our best to hang onto the top 25 per cent? Or maybe fire the bottom 75 per cent, close ranks, reduce the overhead and wheel and deal with a tightly knit organization?

No sir. We have spent a lot of money getting those forty agents together, and we are going to make the whole operation pay, or else. We are going to end up with a winning team, miraculously with the entire forty, but probably with a lot less.

To start, we pay a little more attention to how the top 25 per cent does it. We think we know, but do we? They are all self-starters who do their own thing with little help from management——we don't spend much time with them, because they are too busy working in the right way, making money.

We are going to pick the brains of the top 25 per cent, so to speak. Carefully examine all the agreements they generated for the past year, and get the pattern. You will undoubtedly find that there has been a lot of countersigning, indicating that these people didn't take no for an answer; they pressed on between vendor and purchaser to success.

Notice their personal work habits, which will run to a pattern. They always take advantage of the maximum company policy on advertising, because they know maximum exposure produces maximum sales. They will usually be the first ones in the office, get through their M.L.S. listings and out on the road inspecting the ones they think their buyers would wish to see.

They don't hang around the coffee room reading the paper, doing the crossword puzzle or talking needlessly.

Everything they do in the office is business oriented—aimed at maximum deposits in the bank.

You will notice that they are the ones with the appointment book jammed with entries, and also the ones with the most calls. It is quite common to see them at a messy desk—they are too busy generating business to clean it up.

Well, how do we get the 75 per cent to get cracking like the top producers? Do we start with the bottom 25 per cent, or work our way down with the 50 per cent?

Start with the real losers, the ones who haven't had a deal for about three months. It doesn't matter if they have had ten or fifteen years' experience—as far as you are concerned they have a proven record of being losers. They are costing you money and putting nothing on the plate, so you are faced with a simple fact, shape them up or ship them out.

We often find that non-producers have many personal problems that certainly affect their work habits. They are ducking creditors, so avoid the office where they will have to answer the telephone. Family problems. Problems with alcohol, or gambling. If an experienced agent isn't producing, there is something there, so dig for it. Unless, of course, he is burnt out and tired of it all, which is the end of the road for some who were once so good they put us all to shame.

When you suddenly call a loser into your office, he knows what the meeting will be all about, and he will go to your office with his head swimming with excuses and/or stories about the big deal he is generating. Now is *not* the time to hammer him with the obvious. Now is the time to make him feel at ease so that you can get some sense out of him. It is better to quietly ask him to join you for a cup of coffee, *away from the office* where you and he will be unobserved by other salesmen. If others see you two in a session in your office, they will immediately suspect what it is all about—and some damn fool may even feel smug about it.

Listen to your agent. Feel him out. Let him talk. Perhaps something is bothering him that you can help him with, something totally unrelated to work that is affecting his work. If you can help him, help him. You don't have to hold his hand, but give him a fair shake.

If you can gain his confidence, and convince him that you really do want to help him, you have made a great stride forward. Now you quietly go about ensuring that he:

- Starts his day at nine or sooner——in the office
- Finishes with his M.L.S. and coffee by ten
- Inspects at least three properties by twelve
- Takes advantage of your advertising policy and is in the office during the evening of his advertising
- Makes twenty cold calls a day on the telephone, and five or ten in person in his area
- Pays attention to his ad calls, and services them with energy and sincerity
- Keeps himself looking sharp, with a clean car

This is just for openers. Watch him quietly, encourage him, give him some leads to follow and quietly make sure he does it.

The one thing you must be most careful about——*don't hammer a loser*. All it will do is get his resentment juices flowing. You are trying to make a winner out of him, and blasting with a cannon won't do it.

One of the best sales training films you can show so-so producers is the one available from the Canadian Real Estate Association, titled "Pour it On," starring Bobby Hull. I recommend this film highly. Show it and ask your agents to make notes of the sales points in the film—— then show it ten days later and ask them to note the ones they missed the first time. The result will surprise you, and them.

If you can't move the loser to a better production record, you will just have to face facts and replace him. But do it nicely, because if he wants to stay in real estate he will work somewhere else, and it's always a good policy to leave the door open to business with everybody. Perhaps some day he may have the property one of your buyers wants, and if he leaves on a good note, he'll cooperate with you. As you cast your bread upon the waters, etc.

With the middle 50 per cent, you try to improve their performance by showing a bit more sincere interest in what they are doing. Individually, and collectively. This is your largest group, and the ones with the most promise.

The most important thing a sales manager can accomplish is a sincere dose of rapport with his sales force. Without it, *you* may as well leave, because without rapport, a sales manager will never realize maximum effort from the sales staff. And that's a fact.

Remember, the best salesmen seldom make the best sales managers, and the best sales managers seldom make the best salesmen. Management, unfortunately, very often doesn't realize this. If a broker has a sales manager who has the trust, confidence and rapport of his sales force, he is, indeed, most fortunate.

How are things in your office?

25

Pairing the Agents

How can two agents effectively work together and share *everything* they do on a 50/50 basis? It can be done, and if done properly it can produce financial wonders.

There are probably thousands of real estate salesmen in Canada who are not producing what they *could* produce. Maybe you have a couple in your own office? All that many of them need is a real challenge, and that challenge quite often can be placed just where and how they want it by having a partner.

A salesman who is a self-starter is a person who understands discipline. A self-starter is not a lazy agent, but one who has the discipline to get up and go. He plans his work and works his plan, as the old saying goes, without anyone telling him to get off his ass and get cracking.

So what about the non-self-starters, the thousands of agents who are prone to just coast along? They need a challenge.

Take two such agents in your office. Two that appear to get along well together. Two of socially compatible backgrounds. Ask them to try an experiment in bettering their income by working together as a team. Here are some suggestions for their guidelines.

The first thing they must clearly understand is that you are asking them to do it voluntarily, that they are under no pressure to do it, that you have their best interests at heart in asking them to try something that could change their entire outlook on their work and rewards.

The voluntary agreement to pairing should be for a minimum period of three months, and it must be strictly understood that once the agreement is made, the rewards of everything each one does will be shared by his partner all the way.

When agreement is reached, each one should reveal at the outset what he has been working on, because this will not be shared by the other. The past work of each will be cleaned up, and from then on every phone call, listing, showing, etc. will be a part of the team.

There will be no more wandering in and out of the office with no guidance or responsibility. No more sleeping in and arriving at 10 a.m. to pick up the listings, have a coffee and buzz off for a couple of beers and lunch. (Beer at lunch is a bad habit anyhow——it makes you loggy in the afternoon and gives you bad breath.) From square one the partners will sit down and plan their work together; assess the best areas of mutual production and go to work. It will be a full day from now on.

Their office day starts at 8:45, not 9:30. They will go through the listings first and mutually agree on what the softest and best sales could be. They will inspect together, and keep records and copies of their inspected listings separated from other listings.

They will select an area for listings and assault it. Stick to the area as much as possible. Become experts in the area. They will list together.

The showings will be done individually. Appointments will be shared to help each other with the work load.

At the end of their first week of persistent, concentrated work, they will sit down and see just what has been accomplished——and, you know, they will be amazed to find that they have done in one week what would have taken about three on their own.

It is very important that they be open, honest and frank with each other. I have known of very successful partnerships like this that have broken up because one of the partners began to feel that he was doing more work than the other. No mention was made of it until the feeling turned to resentment and the lid blew off a very nice financial pot. This is the one danger point. Each must ensure that he is not letting the other down, and that he is carrying his full share.

When you have a couple of your agents spending too much time reading the paper, drinking too much coffee, taking too much time off, not calling the office often enough, not being in the office on the day their ads appear, and otherwise frittering away their time and your money, try pairing them.

And if you are a salesman who is wondering why you aren't as good as you think you are, suggest a partnership with another salesman.

Pairing agents can turn losers into winners.

26

The Sales Meeting

The basic objective of a sales meeting is to provide the agents with help and guidance to make more sales, and the quality and class of a meeting can often be judged by attendance.

When salaried sales staff are advised of a meeting, they attend, if for no other reason than the one paying their freight told them to be there.

But a real estate sales manager's meeting can be something else. I remember, about fifteen years ago, being ticked off because I was late for a meeting, with the pointed observation "only those who make $25,000 a year don't have to attend this meeting." But it was interesting to note that the ones making that kind of bread were always there. On time. Successful agents will attend meetings because they know that one good idea or tip from the meeting could fatten the bank roll.

Why do some real estate salesmen avoid meetings? Very basically, it is because the meetings are dull and some individuals haven't been producing and feel a bit "unwanted." All the producers are smiling; the non-producers have nothing to smile about, and their fellow agents know it.

The business world can be a cold world, and unfortunately for those who do not understand that, it has to be. The salesmen who goof off and miss your sales meeting are not doing themselves, or you, any good. Their sales record should be analyzed, because if they are not producing, their absence will be doubly noticed. Non-producers thumbing their noses at you? Surely you don't want them around just to fill up a desk.

Or maybe it is your fault, Sales Manager. Are your meetings dull and uninteresting? Do you ramble through a few listings at your weekly meeting and call it a day?

The first requisite of a sales meeting is to have it start early, and have it start *on time*. I have actually heard of

meetings that start at 10:00 a.m. And why ten? Parents
have to get the kids off to school, so they can't make it by
9:00. Do these agents or their sales managers think for
one minute that any *business* organization is going to have
its employees start at 10:00 because of the children? Everybody is there—on time. And I might add that the worst
thing that can happen is for the sales manager to be late
for his own meeting.

Well, assume we have a self-disciplined group with a
good sales manager. What kind of meetings will be conducted? How? What preparation is needed? What goes
on? I recommend three types for real estate offices:

• Bi-monthly pep meeting
• Weekly sales meeting
• Daily meeting for losers

The bi-monthly pep meeting is to generate enthusiasm
and cement a spirit of teamwork with all employees. Don't
restrict this meeting to salesmen—everybody attends
except a switchboard operator and perhaps one good
agent to look after the store.

Have the bi-monthly meeting away from the office. A
breakfast meeting is best, and start it no later than 8:30.
Don't be cheap. Use the services of a good restaurant, a
social club or hotel.

Prepare the agenda for the meeting well in advance. It
must be conducted by management or the sales manager
in a forceful and interesting manner—otherwise it will
fall flat, and all you'll get out of it is a bill for the breakfast. Here are some suggestions:

In the public schools today they have "show and tell"
days. Make this a part of your bi-monthly meeting. Show a
good sales film, and remind your people how the message
will affect them in their work.

Tell how one or two of your agents turned in an especially good deal and show them you appreciate it by a
token of your appreciation. Be original with your gifts—
40 oz. bottles of booze may be okay, but better than
that would be metric tapes, calculators, top-rated pens,
briefcases, dollar coins, etc. Remember that this meeting
is to create enthusiasm, so *do not* bring any criticism
with you.

Introduce newcomers and don't stop at their names. Tell a little about their background, because this will generate a new friendship or two immediately with some of your agents who will find they have something in common with the new agent.

Whoever is conducting the meeting shouldn't hog the whole floor. Spread it around and get others involved— primarily in advance. Have something arranged beforehand with two or three others but make it look spontaneous. However, the one conducting the meeting must have complete control of it at all times.

This meeting is where new, long range company policies will be introduced.

If you have material for all, ensure that it is placed on chairs before the meeting begins, in sealed envelopes marked "not to be opened before meeting." This saves time in the meeting—no passing papers all over the place.

Ensure the microphone, projector and other aids are tested before the meeting.

End the meeting on a happy, enthusiastic and cheerful note. Let everybody know, sincerely, that you appreciate their efforts and attendance.

The weekly sales meeting is your working meeting, and it is here that you can ensure that you will get those extra deals.

Start it at 9:00 sharp. No later. Have your program all set and know just what you are going to do. Nothing is more discouraging to agents than to go to this meeting and have the manager fumble around with no self-direction, hoping that some good will come out of it. Here are the basics:

Have a list of current office listings available for everybody. Go through them one by one and have the listing salesman bring everybody up to date on the listing.

Have a list of *must-be-sold* listings available. This will include your own and other brokers' listings, where the vendor is panting for an offer. It is very important to have this list—nothing is easier to sell than something that *has* to be sold.

Have a list of new listings available. For this list ensure that agents who work the area inspect the listings and turn in a brief opinion of the price, etc. A sharp sales manager will ensure that the agents inspect new listings by inspecting some of them along with others.

On one open house inspection I had, there were eighty-seven agents through the house. Four sales managers and their salesmen made up more than half the number. They didn't waste their time yapping about the weather, they went through the property, asked a few pertinent questions, made notes and left, to go on to another inspection.

These sales managers were smart cookies. They made sure the salesmen did their homework and got them through the properties whether they liked it or not.

There is an awful lot of laziness in many real estate salesmen. All some of them need is a manager to prod them (in an inoffensive manner) into working. These four managers simply told their agents that they were going to inspect this, and this, and this, with the manager, and away they went. A member of one of the groups sold the property.

Make the weekly meeting interesting. Toss around a few "silver" dollars to those saying the magic word, as Groucho did. Have a small gift for the top agent of the week; a dictionary, a letter opener, a pen set, etc. It won't cost much, and it keeps the meeting moving.

Ensure that you have at least one educational point for the agents. Give each a copy and ask them to maintain a file for the weekly subjects. There is always *something* you can teach your group, and always something interesting they would like to hear. Keep the subject short. Don't be boring.

Time the meeting to last one hour——no more. This will give your group time to inspect properties during the rest of the morning, which is when they should be inspected.

If you have had a lousy week forget it——and look ahead. There is nothing less inspiring than a sour-pussed sales manager.

———————

The daily meeting for losers is a half-hour session you have with just that——losers, non-producers.

There is little excuse for a non-producer in a good moving housing market. *A house salesman who is working has to make deals.* So most of the losers aren't working, aren't doing what they are supposed to be doing. If you have consistent losers, you know what you should do with them, but before you do, ensure that you have done everything you can as their sales manager to help them succeed. You know what they said about leading that horse to water.

Industrial, Commercial and Investment (I.C.I.) real estate people are different. I remember one old gent who didn't produce a nickel's worth of business for almost two years. Kept to himself. We rarely saw him. He was supposed to "know people." At the end of this long dry spell, in one forty day period, he turned in two deals that realized $160,000 in commissions.

If you have a mature, experienced I.C.I. agent who is not leaning on you for draws and seems to know what he is doing, don't worry too much about him. He'll come through. Everybody wants a crack at the big deals, but they are few and far between, as we all know, and if one of your house salesmen aspires to this work, ensure that he is fully aware of the pitfalls. It is the most frustrating area of real estate. Losing a house listing is one thing, but losing a million dollar deal? Ouch.

Be pleasant. Dress well. Look sharp. Set a good example for all.

27

Duty Day

Who looks after the store? The switchboard operator?

We have all experienced this. Visited a broker's office and found no one home. Empty desks all over the place. No licensed agent to handle the situation.

It's great to have everyone out hustling and doing their thing, but every office with a half dozen or more agents certainly should have a duty day roster, and the ones on the list should be responsible enough to do their part by being where they are supposed to be, serving the needs of the public and fellow agents on their day.

If duty agents can't make it because of important appointments or illness, they should switch with others. Shuffle the cards and don't let the team down.

A prevalent ho-hum attitude for duty day personnel is that "you get all the hot buyers." Well, believe it or not, buyers do walk in right off the street, and if there is no one there to look after them, they walk right out again, and take their business with them.

There is no point in telling the receptionist that, "If I'm needed I'll be at home, or at Joe's." Duty day means being physically on duty in the office where one should be. On duty.

The duty agent gets all the walk-in buyers, but what about the walk-in or phone-in sellers? Now, there's something a lot of arguments have gone on about. There are two ways to handle this, and you can take your pick.

The agent on duty gets *everything* that walks in or phones in on that day, or gets all the buyers and a piece of the action on the sellers.

Many offices will have a roster of names for the specific purpose of listing leads. An excellent way to handle this in the case of seller leads is to split the listing with the one on the roster and the one on duty. Two to a listing. If the roster name happens to be the duty name, then move to the next name on the roster, who will split it with the duty staffer.

When there are two to a listing, offers will probably be presented by just one of them, the one available. If the offer is accepted on presentation, then the listing agent who presented the offer should get a bit extra. After all, that's who did the work in getting the deal. If there are sign-backs, the same one would stick with the offer and see it through.

Everybody gets the same treatment, so there can be no soreheads about who got what.

If you are on duty and have to go out with a walk-in or phone-in, then you should try and get someone else to mind the store for you while you are away. The one doing this would then get the walk-ins, etc. during the time he or she is holding the fort.

Duty day gives you time to really clean up your desk and get the cobwebs out of the way. After all, you won't be swamped with inquiries, so you'll have time for the office work. It is also a good excuse to spend a lot of time on the telephone. The business telephone, that is, with old clients and canvassing.

Remember, if someone walks in that door, they did it for a reason, and the reason could very well result in a few thousand dollars in your pocket that might have gone somewhere else.

Don't leave an office vacant with no one in charge. It not only doesn't look good, it is not good business.

28

The Office Listing

The office listing is one that is turned in by management—an executive of the company or perhaps the broker. It can come from anywhere, but it comes from management to the office. A listing received through the mail is also an office listing, because the mail goes to management and management hands it over.

A listing received by telephone by the sales manager is also an office listing.

The exception would be where duty day gives the duty agent all or part of a listing from a walk-in or phone-in on their day.

Well, who gets the office listing? Does the sales manager swipe it? Give it to one of his pals? No. No. No. There are two ways to go with this listing:

- It can be given to an agent on a listing roster, or
- It can be given to nobody

The obvious reason for a listing roster is to ensure that everyone gets a fair share of the goodies, and also to ensure that *someone* is going to be responsible for servicing it.

With a roster, it is better to hand over office listings to a team of two agents, rather than one. The reason for this is that if single agents received the listings, it may be a long time before the roster reaches the last name on the list. So split the listing. Now you have two agents responsible for it.

The reason for giving it to nobody is to provide a little competition in the office. The one who comes up with the accepted offer is also the one who gets the listing commission. This system can often make them move. One person gets it all—listing and sale.

However, there are two slight drawbacks to the foregoing. Someone has to do the physical work and list it in the first place, so if the sales manager doesn't feel so inclined (they do get busy sometimes), he can look around the

office for a salesman who is hungry and send *him* out. But
not for nothing. Let's be fair. If no one is to get the listing
unless he sells it, then the one who did the legwork
should be compensated.

The other drawback is that if the listing is not sold
within a reasonable length of time it is obviously overpriced. Then the agents get tired of it, and nobody goes
near it. Then the vendor gets mad.

So the good old sales manager has to step in and show
his stuff. Reduce the price, and get a little action going on
it. Nobody else will want to be bothered because there is
no listing commission for them.

Take your pick, but the listing roster is really the better
system. It ensures that there is a person responsible for
the listing other than the sales manager, someone the
vendor can get after, someone the sales manager can
blame if it doesn't move, someone to get others moving to
get the listing commission, someone to advertise it, and
someone who maybe needs the money. It also spreads the
cash around the office.

29

Advertising

The new broker, anxious to succeed in the new and proud venture, is often prone to get carried away in one particular area of the operation. So much so that the business stumbles, or worse, fails, and the broker finds himself back at square one wondering what happened.

This area is *advertising*.

The advertising area of a broker's overhead can kill the venture if it is not strictly controlled. A broker *must budget advertising*.

When one considers advertising at, say, $5.00 a line, fourteen lines to an inch, it doesn't take much arithmetic to see $350 for a five inch column of advertising. Add a logo to the top of the advertisement, and there goes another fifty bucks!

The broker in large urban areas is penalized in this respect. To find a buyer in a large area one will advertise in a daily newspaper at a price that seems exorbitant compared to the cost of finding the buyer in a much smaller community. The newspaper circulation dictates the cost, and despite the fact that perhaps 99.99 per cent of city circulation may go to readers who are not interested in what we are offering, the only way to reach our buyer in the paper is to wade through this 99.99 per cent hoping that we can attract the ones we want.

There is a large gap between what a broker would *like* to spend on advertising, and what the broker can *afford* to spend. Which is why it must be strictly controlled by a budget.

The new broker does not really know how well the business will do during the first year, so an affordable or arbitrary figure must be used. There would be little point in going all out *hoping* that the business will be there to cover the expense.

When an annual budget is set, the first step is to consider where the budgeted money will go. (Unfortunately for the budget, the newer the business, the more one must spend to become known, which is probably why we see so many new logos heading the columns.)

There are two considerations in allocating the budget: time and media.

Time is the month. Gear your advertising to a chart following the dollar volume of sales as reported by your real estate board. For example, this chart covers one year as reported by the Toronto Real Estate Board:

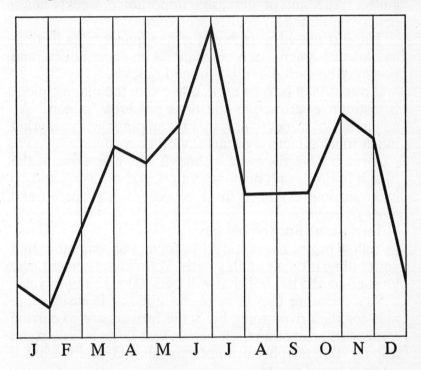

J F M A M J J A S O N D

The money would be wisely spent to match the high and low periods of the sales volume illustrated.

Following this, the highest allotment would be for the month of June, and the lowest for January. It is a common sense approach following the trend of business volume.

Money can be wasted by spending heavily in a lagging period, and failing to take advantage of a good one.

In the budget, include a reserve, or contingency fund. This is to be used for unexpected opportunities to promote those delightful listings we hadn't counted on, or to be used as a cushion to offset the effect of a downtrend when expenses should be reduced.

Media, of course, refers to the area of advertising. It will show how much to spend on each medium, the cost, when the advertising will run and what is to be advertised. We have newspapers, direct mail, radio, television, yellow pages, signs, magazines and public transit.

In newspaper advertising, remember its many areas— daily, weekly, supplements, suburban, college, foreign language, trade, and of increasing importance, weekly newspapers published by real estate boards.

The distinct advantage of the newspaper is its flexibility. Advertisements can be changed on short notice, and size may be varied and positioned quickly.

If direct mail is to be used, make sure the mailing piece is distinctive, attractive and does not look "cheap." An advantage of direct mail is that it can pinpoint the market much more effectively than any other medium.

A radio advertisement, although standing alone at the time it is aired, with no competition, is short-lived, and, to make an impression, it must be very well prepared and *aired frequently*.

Television? For the big guys.

Yellow pages. Everybody uses them, but remember that your billing is on a monthly basis. Your advertisement may look good at $100 but that will be $100 x 12 thank you.

Signs: Ensure that your phone number is easily readable for the driver going by. Some brokers are so carried away with promoting their names that there is little room left for the telephone number, which is really what a curious buyer wants.

Magazines: Here is an area where one can be very selective in reaching the type and financial class of the buyer we want.

Public transit: The back of a bus is hard to beat!

Don't fall into a lazy trap of using the same medium over and over again. Be imaginative. For example, if a house is listed in an area of Chinese residents, consider advertising it in a Chinese newspaper—in Chinese. This may be much more productive and certainly less costly than using a large daily.

In other words, try to avoid paying for unproductive circulation.

Take advantage of the advertising suggestions offered by large daily newspapers, and by your real estate board. They can provide imaginative ideas that produce results and save money.

Develop a slogan and logo which will identify you. Most successful brokers use them, and some are outstanding.

Don't forget the advertising on balloons for the kids, matches for father, and emery boards or rain capes for mother.

When the happy home owners move in, advertise. And what better way than to present the couple with a basket containing a loaf of French bread, a little salt, and a bottle of wine. That's class! (It is also a 2,000-year-old custom.)

Part Three

THE BUSINESS

30

Is Real Estate a Profession?

Is the business of real estate a *profession*?

The *Reader's Digest* dictionary tells us that the noun "profession" is an occupation that involves mental rather than manual labor, especially one of the three learned professions—law, medicine, theology.

The adjective "professional" pertains to an occupation pursued for gain. (I could make a few snide remarks about some occupations pursued for that gain, but I won't bother.)

So, is a real estate broker a professional person or a corporate body? What about a real estate salesperson?

We just can't say one is a professional in his field if he chases after money, so to give credence to the answer I rely on none other than our Tax Review Board.

A corporate real estate broker had, for many years, filed income tax returns on a cash basis. A few years ago the government took a look at this and decided it was the wrong way, saying the broker should have been filing on an accrual basis. So the broker was re-assessed.

The difference in the two filing systems is very basic.

A cash basis means that all the income received and all the bills paid in the taxation year are what is reported.

The accrual basis means that in addition to the foregoing, any billing done for future payment and bills not paid during the taxation year will be reported as credits and debits.

Well, the real estate brokerage didn't think much of the government's attitude, so it appealed. Part of the appeal's successful outcome hinged on whether or not the broker could be defined as being a professional body within the meaning of the Income Tax Act at that time.

The Act included corporate entities as well as individuals as "persons" within its meaning, so we shall treat all brokers the same whether corporate or individual. And so we should, because all brokers operate under identical licensing provisions.

The chairman of the review board made a brief historical reference to the use of the term "profession." He observed that it was well established and one could almost take judicial notice that in the years prior to World War II the term applied almost exclusively to the medical and legal professions.

He said "the term was jealously guarded by them and in my belief still regarded by them as their true description and that they are the only true professions in existence in modern-day society." Boy, talk about ego trips!

For decades, the term "professional" has been adopted by businesses and trades that formerly "would not have been allocated such a lofty position in the business world," to quote the chairman.

However, the board observed it would be a distortion to say that the term extends to the activities of a commercial traveller.

Law dictionaries and even American sources were quoted. Our Parliament, which is loaded with lawyers, didn't care to define the term. And the board said, "It is not for this board or a court of law to seek any unusual meaning for the term."

The decision was in favor of the broker, noting that it was indeed engaged in a profession within the meaning of the Income Tax Act.

Today, anyone engaged in a professional practice must use the accrual method in filing income tax returns. But not a real estate broker, who may use the cash method because it is engaged in work performed on a commission basis.

Confusing? You betcha!

31

What Is a Realtor?

Thousands of signs all over Canada have the word "Realtor" on them. Here is what it means:

We must first start by defining real estate, which is landed property. And landed property is just land. Nothing else.

When something is built on land, it is then called real property, which is land and houses, barns, fences, etc. Combine the words "real" and "property" and you get: "Realty."

Now we go to the "ee" which designates the receiver of whatever is being given; a mortgagee, for example, receives the mortgage as the lender. The "or" designates the giver, such as a donor, vendor, grantor and so on.

So a realtor could logically be defined as one who is giving, or providing, a service in realty, or real property. True, but with some variation.

The word "Realtor" was first used in 1916 in the U.S. and registered by the U.S. Patent Office after World War II by the National Association of Real Estate Boards. The Association exercises legitimate control over the use of the word for the "brokerage of real estate, industrial brokerage, farm brokerage, mortgage brokerage, in the appraisal of real estate, management of real estate, in the building of structures on real estate, in the subdivision of real estate properties, and for consultative and advisory services in community planning for the development of raw land and slum clearance areas."

In 1958 the Canadian Association of Real Estate Boards filed an application for registration of the word "Realtor" as a certification mark and used similar examples of services in its application. The Canadian government examiner of this application referred to a *Webster's* dictionary which defined Realtor as "a real estate broker who is an active member of a local board having membership in the National Association of Real Estate Boards, an organization incorporated in 1908 for the advancement of the interests of real estate brokers and the protection of the public from unprincipled agents or brokers."

This prompted the examiner to decide that the word "Realtor" did not appear to be registrable in Canada. The objection was overcome by pointing out that the entry in the dictionary did not suggest that the word was part of the common language. It was further noted that the definition restricted the use of the word to a real estate broker who is an active member of a local board having membership in the National Association of Real Estate Boards.

Furthermore, the dictionary was published in the U.S., and it was relevantly noted that the trademark "Realtor" had been registered in the U.S. Patent Office (and not in Canada).

In 1960, Canadian Trade Mark Registration No. 117,275, "Realtor," was granted to the Canadian Association of Real Estate Boards (now the Canadian Real Estate Association). The mark has actually been in use in Canada since 1921.

A stringent requirement for ownership of a certification mark is that it may be adopted and registered only by one who is not engaged in the performance of services such as those in association with which the certification mark is used. However, the owner of the mark may license others to use it in association with these services.

Therefore, in Canada, "Realtor" is not a person or corporation. Realtor refers to a standard of service provided by members of the Canadian Real Estate Association, and the dictionary definition put it succinctly when it said, "for the protection of the public from unprincipled agents or brokers."

This is not to say that brokers who are not members of the Canadian Real Estate Association are unprincipled; what it does say is God help any members who are.

It has a very strict code of ethics.

32

It's Tougher Down South

I am beginning to think that a real estate agent in Canada
has a pretty soft touch compared to his or her American
counterpart.

The broker here struggles through his agreement of
purchase and sale, doing his best to help the buyer and
seller reach harmonious accord. When he has the deal,
what's left for him to do?

Sometimes he merely completes a sales record sheet,
reports the sale to his real estate board, sends a copy of
the agreement to solicitors for both parties and deposits a
check in his trust account. Then he keeps his fingers
crossed until payday——the day the deal closes.

When the lawyers for buyer and seller report that the
conveyance has been made, about the only thing left for
the agent to do is disburse the trust funds and head for the
bank with his commission. Sometimes he will have to
chase a seller for the balance of a commission agreement——but that's another story.

Of course, he can do a lot of running around. Such as
when he has to arrange a mortgage or move another
house to cement the deal. But generally speaking, it's a
piece of cake compared to the agent across the border.

In Florida, for example, a broker can go right through
with everything including closing the transaction. When
he has the deposit money in trust (binder in escrow, they
call it) he has three closing statements to work on——one
for the buyer, one for the seller and one for the broker's
own cash reconciliation. All payments are made by the
broker with his principals' money.

The statements will show debits and credits for such
things as payments made to adjust and/or pay off mortgages, insurance, taxes, recording of land and mortgage
deeds, attorney's fees, costs for survey and title insurance,
and a lot of incidentals.

When Florida government inspectors walk in, the whole picture is there. It will show what happened to every penny of the buyer's and seller's money, in detail.

Our inspectors also see what happens to trust money, but usually there are just two parties concerned with it——the seller and the broker. In Florida, checks are flying all over the place——right down to $4 for a documentary stamp.

Mortgage companies in Florida also require something called a "pest inspection"——so the broker naturally rounds up the certificate. And they require a survey, which the broker arranges——and pays for.

The mortgage lender will also demand a title insurance policy or you don't get the money. The broker handles all the details, including payment for the policy.

Title insurance is a big thing in the U.S., a guarantee of sound title to property. If something happens to upset it, the insurer pays the lender his money.

I like the idea of title insurance. It is indemnification against title losses, whether arising out of matters of public record or matters not of record——such as forgery, fraud, concealed marriages, etc.

The insurer may be anyone who has an interest in real estate, including home owners, mortgage lenders, industries and leaseholders.

Under the terms of a title policy, should the title be attacked, the insurance company will defend it in court at its own expense.

However, the Ontario Law Reform Commission didn't think that title insurance was such a hot idea here because it observed that when the insurer investigated before assuming the risk, it usually excluded claims revealed by the investigation.

Well, of course it would. An insurer would be nuts to guarantee title with claims against it before the claims were resolved.

The policy, insuring against forgery, fraud and misrepresentation, is the reason millions of Americans swear by it.

33

The Oklahoma Offer

One of the meanest financial flim-fams devised and used by money-grabbers is the "Oklahoma Offer."

It is slick, professional and to the untrained eye hard to spot. It enables one to purchase property with nothing down and make a substantial and immediate cash profit.

Unfortunately, it leaves a vendor (property seller) stuck with a mortgage, most of which is not worth the paper it is written on. If you are selling a property, watch for it—here is an example of how it works (taken from a small land deal):

- Purchase price: $47,000
- Deposit with offer: $2,000
- Purchaser agrees to pay vendor $30,000 on closing
- Vendor agrees to hold second mortgage for $15,000
- Purchaser agrees to arrange, at his own expense, a first mortgage of not less than $30,000

The innocent vendor adds it up:

Deposit:	$ 2,000
Cash:	30,000
Mortgage:	15,000
TOTAL:	$47,000

If the offer is accepted, the purchaser can go to work and arrange a first mortgage of not $30,000 but $40,000. Remember, it was agreed that the first mortgage will be *not less than $30,000.*

Out of this $40,000 first mortgage, the purchaser will pay the vendor the agreed $30,000, give himself $2,000 to get back the deposit, and put $8,000 profit in his pocket. Need proof?

- First mortgage: $40,000
- Second mortgage: 15,000

                                           $55,000
- Purchase price: 47,000

- Profit to buyer: $ 8,000

The vendor, having agreed to hold a second mortgage of $15,000, is now in the unenviable position of having $8,000 of the $15,000 mortgage *exceed* the purchase price of the property.

If the purchaser is a corporate shell with no assets, it could then walk away with the $8,000 profit and forget the property.

If the vendor (now the second mortgagee) ended up owning the property again, he would owe $40,000 to a first mortgagee. Here is the spot he would be in:

- Property worth: $47,000
- Owing: 40,000

- Equity worth: 7,000
- Cash received: 32,000

                                           $39,000
- Selling price: 47,000

- *Net loss to vendor*: $ 8,000
  (plus headaches and legal fees)

What this means, of course, is that it will cost the vendor (mortgagee) $8,000 out of his own pocket to regain possession of the property.

This money-making scheme is triggered by a clause in the agreement that will allow the purchaser (mortgagor) to increase the principal amount of the first mortgage "without necessarily applying the increase to reduce the principal amount of the second mortgage," which allows the purchaser to arrange and secure the $40,000 mortgage.

If questioned on this noxious point, a glib person will say something to the effect that money obtained from such an increase will be required to improve the property, resulting in greater security for the second mortgagee (vendor). Which is hogwash! Watch it!

Also, the purchaser may ask to assign the agreement to a third, unnamed party. This will release the purchaser from his covenant, and the assignee could be a corporate shell with no assets.

And, in *any* agreement of purchase and sale, here are two warning signs:

Be careful about accepting an offer from a buyer who shows the words "in trust" after his name.

"In trust" could be a corporate shell with no money, and when the time comes to close it would be useless to attempt to legally force a closing if the purchaser decided not to close.

It is tantamount to giving the purchaser an option on the property. Therefore, a serious consideration must be the amount of the deposit made with the offer and the length of time to close the sale. If the purchaser defaults, the vendor could retain the deposit money, which should be an amount considered to be fair compensation for the length of time the property was tied up.

When selling an older property, be careful about agreeing to warrant that there will be no municipal or other legal work orders registered against the property on the date of closing.

A sharp purchaser, under such an agreement, could have the property inspected by municipal, fire and building departments resulting in unheard of orders to repair and/or improve the property. The vendor would be stuck with the bill.

Agree only to there being no work orders registered against the property on the date of acceptance of the agreement.

Caveat emptor? Let the buyer beware?

Let the *seller* beware!

And let the agent beware if he knowingly gets involved in an Oklahoma Offer. Sometimes backfires go off with a helluva bang.

34

Banking

Stiffen the check! Get it certified! Have it marked!

Canadian law does not recognize a "certified" check. So what does it mean?

A check is certified "before delivery" or "after delivery."

Before delivery means that the payer will go to his/its own bank and certify it before giving it to the payee.

What the payer is doing, in fact, is simply asking the bank to certify that funds are in the account *at the time of certification*. Remember, nobody has yet presented the check to the bank for payment.

The bank, in its wisdom, will certify the check and immediately remove the funds from the account to a holding account, keeping the money there until the payee presents it for payment.

Well, you might logically ask, if the check has not been presented for payment, what right has the bank to remove the money from the account?

Very simple. The law quite specifically says that the payer may countermand (stop payment) on a check before it is presented to the bank for payment by issuing such instructions in writing to the bank. And the bank must obey.

So, the bank obviously removes the money to ensure that it is still in the bank in case such a countermanding order is given to the bank. If the bank received such instructions from the payer, it would put a "stop payment" order on the account, and when the certified check arrived for payment, payment would be stopped and the funds placed back in the account.

To put it more succinctly, if a $5,000 check were certified before delivery against an account holding $6,000, and the $5,000 were not removed, the payer could presumably drain the account and say ta-ta to the payee who would be stuck with a N.S.F. certified check.

After delivery is a different story. When a payer gives his/its check to the payee, and the *payee* presents it to the

138

bank for certification, the payee is saying to the bank, "Look, I want you to cash this, but I don't want the money now. I want you to promise to pay me later."

So the bank obliges, certifies the check, removes the money from the account and holds the money to honor its commitment to the payee.

The payer cannot countermand (stop payment) on this check because *it has been presented for payment* and the bank has honored the presentation. The funds and payment therefore become a charge on the bank itself which it must honor. It has effectively paid the check but is holding the money until the payee comes back for it.

Summarizing it, a payer can stop payment on a certified check if the payer certified it, and conversely, a payer cannot stop payment on a certified check if it were certified by the payee.

Real Estate Brokers are required by law to have a trust account, which is strictly used to hold money in trust for others.

For example, the money could be rents collected on behalf of property owners who have retained the broker to manage property, or deposits on real estate transactions. Government inspectors keep a watchful eye on the movement of money in and out of the accounts, and woe to the broker who misuses the trust.

But what does a trust account mean to a bank?

It is simply another bank account—which leads one to ask just how secure the money really is in the account. Can a judgment creditor seize the money in a trust account?

A broker will have three accounts in a bank. One for his personal use, one for his general business use, and one for money held in trust. If a sheriff's officer arrived at the bank and produced a notice of seizure to the bank manager to seize the broker's money on behalf of a judgment creditor, what would the bank manager do?

Is your money safe in the trust account?

The bank manager, in his wisdom (and they are pretty smart cookies), would know that the trust account is there to hold money in trust for others, so here is what his response to the sheriff's officer would be:

Money from the broker's personal account *and* his general business account (if it is not a limited company) would be surrendered up to the amount of the seizure. If the broker's personal and general account were depleted by the seizure, what happens to the third account, the trust account?

The trust account is a different matter. The banker would accept the seizure, but would not surrender any money from the trust account. He would, however, put a "hold" on the account.

Whenever the broker wished to write a check on the trust account, he would have to satisfy the banker that the check really was, in fact, someone else's money that had to be paid according to the terms of the trust. Once this was established, the bank would honor the check and release the funds.

If the broker, for example, held a deposit on a real estate transaction for, say, $5,000, and the broker's commission was $4,000, when the sale was completed the broker could write a check for $1,000 to be paid to the vendor, but he could not write one for the $4,000 commission to be transferred to his general account. This portion could be seized by a judgment creditor, because when the sale closed it belonged to the broker.

So you see, money held in trust by a real estate broker is quite safe from seizure.

My brother Charles, a retired Air Force Colonel, once showed me the instrument panel of a CF-101 (Voodoo) aircraft. Staring at the pilot, with stark reality, is a large button stamped with the word "panic." Push this button and there is no turning back. Out you go, parachute and all, and what you leave behind comes crashing down.

With decades of experience in doing business with Canadian banks, I am rapidly reaching the conclusion that newly appointed and "caretaker" bank managers are supplied with these buttons as part of their ration in the kit of new management.

Many of you reading this will recall with horror your own experience with a new manager. Demand loans recalled, overdrafts cancelled, checks bounced and with them your frustration and anger. But you survived.

One of the great strengths in our democratic system of life is the fact that there is another bank across the street waiting for you with open arms after your manager has pushed the panic button and fired you out the front door. One would hope that the banker across the street will be one who is self-assured, competent and with enough business acumen to know when to heave the panic button into the garbage.

A grave business error can be to do all your banking in one bank.

Consider this revelation from a bank customer: "My greatest rapport in banking was reached with a big cigar-smoking Irishman who was the most unflappable manager I had ever encountered. He was so good that when he got promoted, he received a double promotion, which was a sad day in my commercial life.

"My notes were being honored, the overdraft wasn't causing the giant corporation any pain, my checks were being cashed and everything was at peace in my small banking world. Then BANG, BANG.

"It was my custom to drop into the bank on a Friday to pick up a couple of hundred for my wife's weekend shopping and pocket money for the following week. Consider then, my frustration on black Friday when I walked in for my weekly ration and was advised that my overdraft was too high so "hah hah" no money today!

"The annoying part of this was that I had just made a deposit!

"If I had an established account at another bank, there would have been no problem. It is difficult to open an account at a bank at 5:30 on a Friday and immediately ask it for a couple of hundred."

So remember the noun "contingency." Webster's dictionary defines it as "a chance or *possible occurrence.*"

Unless you are Daddy Warbucks, it could happen to you.

Such annoyance can go further than a few dollars of required cash. What about unexpected bills that must be paid? If a bank has decided to cut you off completely until your overdraft has been reduced, it certainly won't honor any of your checks.

So do yourself a favor, and spread your bread. Establish credit at more than one bank! Contingency.

35

The Deemed Reinvestment Principle

Just what is meant by "effective yield," a term commonly used in mortgage lending?

This comes under a mathematical principle of deemed reinvestment, which means that when interest is paid more frequently than once in each twelve-month period, the lender is deemed to immediately reinvest the interest at the same rate as the mortgage contract rate.

To explain, assume a one-year mortgage loan of $100,000 is made at the rate of 10 per cent per annum, with the interest payable in two six-month periods, not in advance. Also assume the principal is not payable until the end of the year.

This loan example, being payable "interest only," does not come under the provision of the Interest Act that says the deed must state the annual rate of interest, calculated yearly or half-yearly, not in advance.

In each of the two six-month periods, the borrower will pay the lender $5,000, for a total of $10,000 by the end of the term. There's the 10 per cent.

But the deemed reinvestment principle is that instead of putting the first six-month payment of $5,000 in his pocket, the lender immediately loaned it to someone else on the same terms.

Therefore, for loaning this $5,000 he receives 5 per cent, or $250 at the end of six months, which is when the first loan is due.

So he received a total of $10,000 from the first borrower, and he is deemed to have received $250 from the second borrower, for a total of $10,250, which is a return of 10¼ per cent on the loan contracted at 10 per cent.

If interest on this loan were to be paid every month, the borrower would pay $833.33 per month, and if it is assumed the lender immediately reinvested the money on

143

the same terms, and did, he would realize 10.47 per cent on his 10 per cent loan.

But there is no guarantee that this lender will reinvest the interest he receives. If he just kept it, he would receive 10 per cent annual interest, no matter how often the borrower paid him.

On the other hand, if the borrower paid the lender with money taken out of an interest-bearing account, it certainly would cost him more than 10 per cent, because he would be deprived of the interest he could have earned on the money he used to make interest payments.

But then again, there is no guarantee that the borrower did use his interest-earning money. If he took it out of a filing cabinet, the loan would cost him 10 per cent per annum, and no more, regardless of how often he paid this lender.

Recently, a borrower in a large (interest-only) mortgage agreed to pay the lender on a monthly basis, being 1/12 of the annual rate. The deed did not mention any frequency of calculating the interest, so the borrower later decided the lender was getting too much money.

He sued on the basis that the interest was calculated and paid monthly, saying that it should have been calculated annually and paid monthly. Which, of course, would have cost less.

He lost. The Supreme Court of Canada, noting that the mortgage said nothing about how the interest was to be calculated, turned down the argument of the deemed reinvestment principle.

Now, far be it from me to criticize a high court decision, but here is what Mr. Justice Anglin of the Supreme Court of Canada said in a 1917 judgment concerning mortgages:

"If the rate be stated to be, say, 10 per cent per annum, although this is not an explicit statement that the interest is to be computed yearly, such a computation is implied, and I should regard it as a sufficient statement to that effect and as precluding the computation of interest on any other than a yearly basis."

No wonder the average guy out there just says "how much do I pay a month?" and lets others worry about the details!

36

Math Muddle

How about some real estate mathematics? We'll start off by pulling a fast one on our calculator:

All listings by real estate boards are now in metric, and an example of the frustration this has caused is for one to convert a rental dollar rate per square foot to a rate per square metre.

To do this quickly, enter the *price* per square foot and assume it is a number of square metres. Then tell your calculator to convert this to square feet and you will get the rate per square metre.

The calculator thinks we are converting to square feet but we're not. Heh heh.

If you don't have a conversion calculator, then do it the old-fashioned way. Take the rate per square foot, divide it by 9.29, multiply by 100, and you have the rate per square metre. Maybe you better do it this way.

Want to know what average rate of interest you are paying on those two mortgages? We'll use simple interest:

1st mtge	$54,000@ 11.5% =	$6,210 per year
2nd mtge	22,000@ 14.0% =	3,080 per year
	$76,000	$9,290

$$\text{Here we go:} \quad \frac{9,290}{76,000} \times 100 = 12.22\%$$

Piece of cake!

So a year ago you paid $107,000 for your house. Now you hear it is worth $118,500. How much has it increased in value?

$$\frac{118,500}{107,000} \times 100 = 110.7 - 100 = 10.7\%$$

Or, do it another way. Take the increase of $11,500, multiply it by 100, divide this by 107,000 and you have the same thing——10.7 per cent.

However, that 10.7 per cent could mean a lot more to you. The dollar increase is $11,500——and let's assume you put $20,000 into the place, including everything. Why, your cash investment has increased in value by no less than:

$$\frac{11,500 \times 100}{20,000} = 57.5\%$$

Oh dear. The market slumped and the value of the darned house went down. You paid $107,000 and now those experts say you'd be lucky to get $100,000 for it. How much of a drop is this?

$$\frac{7,000 \times 100}{107,000} = 6.54\%$$

Well, what happened to that $20,000 you sunk into the place? Oh boy, your investment took a nosedive. Like 35 per cent worth. (Figure it out the same way we did for the drop in the house value.)

There are 2.47 acres in a hectare, and anytime I convert this I gag. Our metric commission says we have it because it is the worldwide way of doing things. Not with hectares, it ain't!

A few centuries ago, an acre was considered to be the amount of land a man with a yoke of oxen could plow in a day. The British Weights and Measures Act of 1878 defined it as containing 43,560 sq. ft., and this "statute acre" was adopted by Canada and the U.S.

However, it is interesting to note that Scotland, Ireland, Wales and even some English counties did not agree with it, and older land measurements of the acre are still to be found in these areas.

In the following countries, I could only find one hectare, and the list is endless:

Country	Unit	Size in Statute Acres
Austria	Joch	1.42 acres
Belgium	Hectare	2.47
Brazil	Cuarta	0.92
Cyprus	Donum	0.33
Denmark	Tonder land	1.36
Egypt	Feddan	1.04
Ireland	Acre	1.62
Russia	Dessiatine	2.70
Scotland	Acre	1.27
Wales	Erw	0.89
Wales	Stang	0.67

When a farmer talks about the "back forty," he means acres. Now he'd have to say the back 16.18745 hectares.

37

Usury

Remember the federal Small Loans Act?

That's the one that drove lenders up the wall with restrictions on loans of $1,500 and less.

Two per cent a month on the first $300, 1 per cent a month on the next $700, and ½ per cent on a balance of up to $1,500.

Away back in 1971, I wanted to know how the act affected mortgage loans, and my inquiry to the Department of Insurance provided some revealing facts.

Real estate and mortgage brokers probably never knew it, but they were considered moneylenders under the Small Loans Act.

This brought them into restrictions in lending $1,500 or less—and, remember, not so many years ago there was a lot of small-mortgage lending going on.

The government took the view that the licensed lending rates under the act should not be applied in the case of mortgage loans, but it also said such loans were to be limited to a rate of 1 per cent per month on balances outstanding.

Therefore, for many years mortgage brokers really should not have created confusion when such loans had blended (principal and interest) payments.

One per cent a month is 12 per cent a year, but it is compounding the interest monthly.

The Federal Interest Act (not the Small Loans Act) says a blended payment mortgage must show the annual rate of interest calculated annually or semi-annually.

So, 12 per cent compounded monthly would have to read 12.682503 per cent in the mortgage to comply with the Act, which would look silly. Wouldn't it?

So I kept my mouth shut.

I mention all this to bring you up to date on the subject.

The other day I was surprised to hear a business commentator remark that there are no government restrictions on usury, or words to that effect.

Usury, of course, is charging and/or extracting unconscionable rates of interest on loans.

This remark caused me to get out my copy of something called Bill C-44, an Act to amend the Small Loans Act and to amend the Criminal Code.

It received royal assent on December 7, 1980.

This Act repealed the Small Loans Act, so it doesn't exist any more.

Mortgage lenders can relax.

In amending the Criminal Code, the Act placed restrictions on what anyone can charge for lending money, and I quote:

Section 305.1 of the Criminal Code says everyone who:

(a) enters into an agreement or arrangement to receive interest at a criminal rate, or (b) receives a payment or partial payment of interest at a criminal rate, is guilty of:

(1) an indictable offence and is liable to imprisonment for five years, or (2) an offence punishable on summary conviction and is liable to a fine of not more than $25,000 or to imprisonment for six months, or to both.

The Act defines "criminal rate" as being "an effective annual rate of interest that exceeds 60 per cent on the credit advanced."

This 60 per cent means the aggregate of all charges and expenses, whether in the form of a fee, fine, penalty, commission or other similar charge or expense.

Regardless of how exorbitant the 60 per cent may be, there are severe penalties for usury in Canada.

Don't believe everything you hear on the radio.

38

Property Rights

Real estate associations are justifiably concerned about the erosion of property rights in Canada.

Before anyone here heard of such a thing, William the Conqueror led the way in 1066 when he set about grabbing all the land in Britain.

Now, taking *all* the land in an entire country is what I call a *real* erosion of rights. Nobody but the king had any say about who would have property rights.

And he didn't fool around. He not only owned the land, but he wanted an inventory of everything. Right down to the number of fishponds.

In 1086, despite great resentment, elaborate accounts of the estates in England were made by panels of the King's commissioners.

From all this inventory, a summary was compiled which became the well known *Domesday Book*

The first attack on Canadian property owners' rights started with day one of Confederation.

The British North America Act of 1867 says all of Canada is held by the Crown-in-right of the provinces.

That means any government agency can kick us off our land any time it pleases—which is quite often.

Recently, the Winnipeg *Real Estate News* put everything but the kitchen sink into a detailed analysis of rights and limits on the subject.

It outlined what it called "some of the more typical restrictions."

Now, I don't know about you, but I certainly am thankful we have some of those restrictions.

When I was a boy, there were no zoning bylaws as such, so every other house on the block had chickens, or rabbits, or ducks; even a pig or two (real pigs). It was a rural street, where everybody did his own thing.

Now we are civilized, so we are told.

Municipal bylaws control the use of land and buildings, so that is one restriction I'll buy——with reservations, of course.

Under the "Rights of Alienation," the *News* pointed out, a landowner has the right to sell or give away his land, but the erosion of these rights is quite considerable.

It can be affected by various provincial Registry Acts, Planning Acts, Land Titles Acts, Land Transfer Tax Acts, Family Law Reform Acts, Mental Health Acts, Construction or Mechanics Lien Acts and others such as: subdivision control, land transfer regulations, special regulations governing the sale of land to non-residents and so on.

Quite a mouthful indeed!

However, arguments can be made in favor of some of them.

If I did a lot of work on a house and didn't get paid, I would certainly be thankful for the Mechanics Lien Act. Before the house could be sold, I would get my money. Simple as that.

A list under "The Right of Possession" points out some interesting erosions: Landlord and Tenant Acts, Environment Protection Acts, Fire and Health Inspection Acts, occupiers liability laws, rent review legislation and laws relating to adverse possession.

Well, again I say: We certainly need some of these. Especially the Fire and Health Inspection Acts. But we sure as hell don't need the vote-getting, highway robbing Landlord and Tenant Acts in their present form.

There is a lot of high-priced talent in organized real estate.

I would like to see it used to do a real number on this subject, pointing out all the *good* things, and all the *bad* things about all erosions of property rights.

39

Some Interesting Real Estate Judgments

Here is some disturbing news for real estate brokers and their salesmen. And how.

Bill Hotshot is a whiz-bang salesman. He turns in about four deals a month and makes plenty.

But old Bill likes the good life and spends the stuff faster than he makes it.

His broker appreciates the business Bill brings in.

So the broker and Bill have a neat little arrangement—a drawing account for Bill. Just a few hundred a week to keep his lifestyle going.

When Bill's deals close, the commission payable to him goes into his drawing account, and Bill carries on with his weekly advances.

While Bill is living the good life, he runs up so many bills that he can't keep up with them.

Then the creditors' judgments start rolling in.

One of these creditors decided to make Bill's broker a garnishee.

This means the creditor has obtained a court order for the broker to hand over Bill's earned commissions until the debt is fully paid.

Bill was into the broker for thousands by this time, but the broker wasn't worried.

He figured all Bill's future earnings could simply be credited to the drawing account, because, after all, Bill did owe the money.

The broker thought he had first crack at Bill's commissions.

A lot of other brokers, I am sure, think the same way about debits and credits in those drawing accounts.

Alas, that sort of thinking is now a no-no. So ruled an Ontario district court.

A debtor was employed by the garnishee as a commission salesman, just like Bill.

The garnishee paid advances to the employee against commissions to be earned by him in the future.

The garnishee said there was no debt owing to the employee because he advanced him $5,000.

The advances were for various expenses paid on behalf of the debtor employee, including credit card payments and moving expenses, but the employee didn't use the money to pay those bills.

The creditor argued that the garnishee, if successful in his submission that no debt was owing, could frustrate garnishment by giving the employee advances.

The employee signed a "ledger card" with his employer, the garnishee, which provided: "I hereby understand and agree that any monies to me are paid only as an advance against potential earnings."

Both the creditor and the garnishee had bona fide claims against the debtor salesman.

The judge said, "I have come to the conclusion that when a commission will be earned by the debtor it will be a 'debt payable' by the garnishee to the debtor, irrespective of prior advances paid by the garnishee and effectively made as draws against commissions to be earned."

Ontario statute law says: "A creditor under an order for the payment or recovery of money may enforce it by garnishment of debts payable to the debtor by other persons."

The judgment found that the garnishee was indebted to the employee when commissions were earned, even though he had made advances.

The employer couldn't automatically take the money. So the creditor was entitled to it.

Caveat Borrower

Do you know that when you sign a mortgage deed you are signing a death pledge?

The word mortgage is composed of two French words, *mort* (death) and *gage* (pledge).

Centuries ago, when a man of property died, his estate went to his eldest son.

When this son needed money, but couldn't wait for father to kick the bucket, he could borrow money against the estate he would some day inherit.

This was done by giving the lender security by signing a mortgage deed.

It was a pledge to pay when the estate became the property of the borrower. The death pledge. Payable upon father's death.

I don't know what the lender would do if the borrower died first. Their new heir, No. 2 son, could tell him to go ta-ta. He signed nothing.

Later versions of the death pledge were that the pledge becomes dead when the debt is paid. Or that the property pledged for the loan becomes dead, or lost, due to failure to pay. Take your pick.

The Ontario Mortgages Act places specific responsibility on just who is liable for repaying the mortgage debt. It starts, of course, with the one who signed the mortgage deed——the original borrower.

If the mortgage has no restrictive convenant affecting the conveyance of the property to a third party, then the borrower (property owner) can sell to a buyer agreeing to assume the mortgage debt.

The buyer then becomes a party to the debt. But the one who signed the deed is still on the hook and responsible for the debt. If the foregoing buyer sells the property, then the new buyer is in the picture and the seller is off the hook. What this all means is that the original borrower and the current owner of the property are both responsible to the lender.

Well now, what happens if one of these later owners goes to the lender and renews the mortgage for a further period of time? And at a higher rate of interest? Is the original borrower still responsible for the debt when such changes have been made, unknown to him?

Well, just such a thing did happen. And the rate of interest in the mortgage was increased by 70 per cent! Believe it or not.

Then the borrower defaulted. He stopped making payments, then conveyed the equity of redemption. The new owner of the mortgage took a dim view of the property owner defaulting on the loan and handing the property over to someone else, so the whole thing ended up in court.

The mortgagee went after the original borrower in the mortgage deed and looked to him for repayment of the debt. Naturally, the defendant objected, saying the mortgage was altered without his consent and was probably shocked at the prospect of repaying such a debt with its huge increase in the rate of interest.

Now, I am sure that a lot of you out there would say that the lender is full of hot air in expecting the original borrower to pay the debt off under such circumstances. Right?

Well, recently the Supreme Court of Ontario said the original borrower in this deal is still responsible for the debt, but only at the original rate of interest shown in the mortgage deed at the time of signing.

Caveat, borrower. That's for sure.

Borrower Be Polite

When I come back to earth in the next world I would like to be a judge.

After pouring over countless judgments on real estate, I have reached an inescapable conclusion: Judges seem to have most of the brains.

For example, I am very familiar with Section 10 of the federal Interest Act. I have written about it, lectured on it, and referred many people to it. It is seared in my brain.

But after all these years, one little item that stands out in Section 10 went right past me. I never caught it. And I'll bet thousands of real estate and mortgage brokers never caught it either.

Laws concerning interest charges go back a lot of years. The first one was a 1777 ordinance in Quebec, which said the maximum will be 6 per cent per annum. This rate was carried into the Upper Canada Act of 1811.

Then the government got generous and the English Act of 1854 repealed the usury statutes and generally left interest rates up to the borrower and lender.

Section 10 (1) of today's Interest Act is the same as it was in 1925, when a Saskatchewan court of appeal made an interesting observation on it. Briefly, the section says that when a mortgage has a term of more than five years, the person liable to redeem the mortgage may pay to the lender the amount due for principal and interest at any time after the expiration of five years.

With this payment, the borrower must pay three months' further interest. Then it says no further interest shall be chargeable, payable or recoverable at any time thereafter (on the mortgage).

We have long-term mortgages available now, so this statute, in favor of the borrower, sounds pretty good. Pay off the mortgage after five years with a reasonable bonus and that's the end of the matter.

Not so.

Sixty years ago the honorable court said: "this section does not give a mortgagor entitled to redeem the right to a discharge on tender of the mortgage monies, or interest, after the expiration of five years from the date of the mortgage.

"There is nothing in the section which says he should be entitled to have the mortgage discharged. Ordinarily, if a mortgagee cannot obtain any further interest, he will take his money and execute a discharge of the mortgage. But the section does not say he must do so."

If you think I am digging up ancient history, forget it. This sixty-year-old precedent was affirmed in 1983 in the B.C. Supreme Court, which said: "It is difficult to understand what use a mortgagee can make of an instrument where payment is made in full. Nonetheless, if he wishes, it seems he may refuse to discharge the mortgage until the date of its maturity."

All the foregoing suggests that a borrower in a long-term mortgage may be well advised to be polite to the lender. If rates take a dive from a high-rate mortgage, the borrower can certainly take advantage of section 10. But it doesn't guarantee the lender will discharge the mortgage.

Which could be damned annoying if a cash buyer came along for the property: he would want a nice, clean title. If the lender won't hand it over, what is the borrower going to do?

Despite the law, the lender did lose a lot of high-rate interest when that mortgage was paid off before maturity, and he's pretty sore about it. Are we going to find borrowers paying hefty bonuses to get that discharge under such circumstances?

And why wasn't the Act amended to take care of this annoying matter? Sixty years is too long to leave some crummy wording on the books!

Buyer Be Careful

A buyer should be especially careful when instructing an agent to prepare an offer to buy a parcel of real estate, regardless of what it is.

A big safeguard one can take is to instruct the agent to include any special features important to the buyer.

I recommend this even if the features about the property are noted on the real estate listing and even if the agent's responses to one's questions are reassuring.

Here are two very good examples of why I say this.

In the first case, a real estate agent listed a parcel of land, was told by the seller that the property was an "apartment site," and the listing showed the property to be "apartment zoned."

The property was actually zoned for single family dwellings, though it was adjacent to land zoned for apartments.

The listing agent did not check the zoning with municipal authorities and forwarded the listing through the M.L.S. system to other agents—with the false zoning information included.

One of the sub-agents received a visit from a buyer who expressed a wish to purchase a lot which was apartment zoned, for building purposes. The sub-agent recommended the listing, but before making an offer, the buyer asked the agent to check the zoning. This the agent did, but not with city hall. He phoned the listing agent who said it was apartment zoned.

Thus assured, the buyer incurred expense by having the property surveyed, removing an existing house and clearing the lot.

Then the roof fell in. The true nature of the zoning was discovered and everybody ended up in court.

The judgment found the sellers liable to the plaintiff (buyer) for fraud and had this to say about the real estate agents: The listing agent was negligent in representing the property to be "apartment zoned" without ensuring it in fact and he and his employer were liable to the plaintiffs.

The same considerations applied to the selling agent even though he was encouraged by the listing agent to believe the property was zoned for apartment construction.

In another example, a couple bought a home which, according to the listing, said cable television was available. After closing the deal, they were told by the cable company that it was not available in their area.

The buyers, after spending more than $900 to have a TV tower erected, sued the agents involved, but lost.

The judge said he accepted the agent's statement that the buyer made no mention of cable television as a priority and observed that the buyer could have protected himself by asking the agent to deliberately check the availability of the service, or have included it in the agreement of purchase and sale.

He also said there was no law cited to suggest there is any duty on a listing or selling agent to check the items listed and there was no guarantee by any of the defendants as to the accuracy of the listing.

I like that part about including it in the agreement. If these home buyers had done this, a lot of time, money and grief could have been saved.

If you spot something on a listing you like, especially if it is partly instrumental in causing you to make an offer, put it in writing.

Make it a part of your agreement of purchase and sale.

You can't believe everything you hear, or see on a listing!

Caveat Agent

A property in Mississauga (near Toronto) was listed, with a commission of 6 per cent to be paid on its sale.

Nothing unusual about that, but eventual litigation over the 6 per cent commission has provided agents all over the country with something to remember.

Several offers on the property were presented, but all were for amounts unacceptable to the seller.

Then, an agent, who wasn't the listing agent, presented an offer to the seller that was within striking distance of a deal.

The seller took the offer to his lawyer, which resulted in a sign-back increasing the price and reducing the term in a purchase mortgage for which the buyer had asked.

The seller also reduced the commission agreement contained in the offer to 5 per cent.

Then the agent took the counter-offer back to the buyer, who accepted it and the transaction later closed.

After closing, the seller's lawyer sent the broker a check which together with the deposit which had been paid to the agent, equalled 5 per cent of the selling price. The agent demanded a further 1 per cent and went to court to collect.

The judge observed the intent of the listing agreement was quite clear; a commission of 6 per cent to be payable on any sale made by the agency during the currency of the agreement. But he also noted the intent of the agreement of purchase and sale was very clear; it provided that the seller's acceptance was made on the basis that the commission would be 5 per cent.

This was the last document signed by the seller before the sale closed, and the agent did nothing to dispute the seller's acceptance on that basis.

The judge said: "The agent could have reminded the defendant of the term of the listing agreement and refused to submit the offer to the purchaser for amendment. Had that occurred, the defendant would then have had to decide whether to accept the offer with the full commission or reject it. That did not occur."

It is here that agents should pause and reflect. The sign-back was accepted by the agent, and the judge noted that "procedures followed within the agency thereafter are of no consequence in this action.

"The listing agreement was superseded by the written terms of the acceptance of the offer to purchase and the plaintiff (agent) is bound by it."

The listing agent and his broker said they did not know of the commission change, but this did not impress the judge, who said: "Irrespective of whether it was the listing agent or the selling agent who presented the counter-offer to the purchasers, the fact remains that the plaintiff, through its agents, acquiesced in and accepted the vendor's terms that the offer was only acceptable to him if the commission were reduced to 5 per cent."

The obvious lesson to be learned here is that a listing agent and/or his broker should certainly follow an offer like a hound dog.

What would have happened here if the selling agent had turned in the deal at 3 per cent?

While agents everywhere will mostly benefit from all this, property owners would also be well advised of what a learned judge has noted:

A 6 per cent listing agreement doesn't necessarily mean the agent is going to get it.

Caveat agent.

40

Big Brother Is Watching You

The Ontario government does not view lightly the registration of real estate brokers and salesmen. Neither do other provincial governments.

There are very strict rules and orders of conduct for the industry contained in the Real Estate and Business Brokers Act. Ditto for mortgage brokers under the Mortgage Brokers Act.

To be fair to all concerned and to ensure that one's licence to stay in business is not arbitrarily cancelled, or registration refused, there is an avenue of appeal open to all. This is known as the Ontario Commercial Registration Appeal Tribunal, which strongly reminds us that: "The real estate industry is one in which major transactions involving large sums, often sums representing people's life savings, are involved. Only persons of complete trustworthiness should be considered suitable for registration." Amen.

Once in a while, an agent will find himself in hot water, either through his own dishonesty as an agent, or as an applicant for registration. If the government registrar of agents decides the agent is not exactly considered to be the type of person to be in possession of a certificate of registration, appropriate recommendations are made to ensure his application is denied.

The hearings on appeal to the tribunal can produce some funny stuff. Here is a letter written by the Assistant Registrar of Real Estate and Business Brokers, to an applicant seeking registration: "We received your application for registration as a real estate salesperson last January. No action was taken since we understood that you appeared in court and were convicted on a charge of conspiracy to import counterfeit money. In view of the fact that you were in jail, we were unable to register you. . . . " Unquote.

So you see, even an applicant with a tainted personal record may have the right to be heard.

In this case, registration was eventually refused under Section 6 of the Act, which says: "An applicant is entitled to registration except where his or her past conduct affords reasonable grounds for belief that he or she will not carry on business in accordance with law and with integrity and honesty." So much for an applicant for registration.

What about those bad apples who already have been registered?

On hearing about any hanky-panky by an agent, the government registrar will move swiftly to ensure the public is protected. The suspect will be hauled up on the carpet and asked to explain himself in view of evidence received. If the explanation has no substance, recommendation may be made to cancel the agent's registration. Then the agent may appeal, a necessary right to ensure all can see that justice is done.

Brokers have lost their tickets for doing something which I am sure they considered to be quite innocent, however stupid it was——such as moving money out of a trust account before a deal closes, one of the really big no-nos in real estate.

A broker needs a little money. He knows one of his deals is as solid as the rock of Gibraltar, one that will definitely close. No doubt about that, he says.

So what's the harm in moving the trust money a couple of weeks ahead of time? He's out of business when his inspector finds out about it, that's what.

41

Requirements for a Licence to Trade in Real Estate

The Quebec government puts it very succinctly: "The primary objective of the Real Estate Brokerage Act is to *protect the public*." The Real Estate Council of British Columbia, established pursuant to the B.C. Real Estate Act, states: "The Real Estate Council's task is to maintain high standards in the conduct of real estate transactions, and to assist the Superintendent of Real Estate in protecting the public."

Protecting the public. That's what licensing is all about.

Every province has statute law controlling the conduct of real estate salesmen and brokers. No more walking in with a few bucks and walking out with a government licence to trade in real estate, like in the old days. Believe it or not!

Every province now requires an applicant who wishes to be licensed to pass written examinations. The requirements vary from coast to coast, but the name of the game is examination——pass it or you don't legally trade in real estate.

Because each province has its own regulations, and because regulations change periodically, it would not be appropriate to cover such a wide range of requirements here.

The people to tell you what current regulations are for becoming licensed agents in all ten provinces are:

BRITISH COLUMBIA: Real Estate Council of British Columbia,
5th Floor, 626 West Pender Street,
Vancouver, B.C. V6B 1V9

ALBERTA:

Superintendent of Real Estate,
Alberta Consumer and
  Corporate Affairs,
19th Floor, 10025 Jasper
  Avenue,
Edmonton, Alberta T5J 3Z5

SASKATCHEWAN:

Insurance and Real Estate
  Branch,
Saskatchewan Consumer and
  Commercial Affairs,
1871 Smith Street,
Regina, Saskatchewan S4P 3V7

MANITOBA:

The Registrar, The Real Estate
  Brokers Act,
Manitoba Consumer and
  Corporate Affairs,
1128-405 Broadway,
Winnipeg, Manitoba R3C 3L6

ONTARIO:

The Registrar,
Real Estate and Business Brokers
  Act,
Ontario Consumer and
  Commercial Relations,
555 Yonge Street,
Toronto, Ontario M7A 2H6

QUEBEC:

Ministere de la Justice
Service du courtage immobilier
  du Quebec,
220, Grande Allée est, #910
Quebec City, Quebec G1R 2J1

NOVA SCOTIA:

The Supervisor, Regulated
  Industries,
Nova Scotia Department of
  Consumer Affairs,
5151 Terminal Road,
P.O. Box 998,
Halifax, N.S. B3J 2X3

NEW BRUNSWICK:	Licensing Supervisor, Department of Justice, New Brunswick Consumer Affairs Branch, P.O. Box 6000, Fredericton, N.B. E3B 5H1
P.E.I.:	The Director, Insurance & Real Estate Division, Prince Edward Island Department of Justice, P.O. Box 2000, Charlottetown, P.E.I. C1A 7N8
NEWFOUNDLAND:	Supervisor, Licensing and Enforcement Division, Newfoundland Department of Consumer Affairs and Communications, P.O. Box 4750, St. John's, Newfoundland A1C 5T7
YUKON:	Superintendent of Real Estate, Consumer, Corporate & Labour Affairs Branch, Yukon Justice, Box 2703, Whitehorse, Yukon Y1A 2C6
NORTHWEST TERRITORIES:	The Justice Department of the Northwest Territories advised that there is no legislation governing real estate agents in the Northwest Territories. The only licensing that may be required would be a municipal license in the community where the agent was carrying on business.

42

Short Pieces

SALES CONTESTS: There was once a large brokerage house with many salesmen. Listings were not what they should be, so the broker offered, for a period of time, $10 cash for every new listing turned in. Cash the *minute* the listing was turned in.

Do I have to tell you what happened? There were so many vastly overpriced listings, the broker almost ran out of $10 bills, so the whole idea, sincere as it was, fell flat on its rump.

Sales contests are great—but one failing with them is to offer a few prizes *at the end of the contest*. What happens is that halfway through the ninety day period or whatever, a few will pull so far ahead of the pack that the rest will simply lose interest in it.

To be effective, contests should have variety and plenty of in-between prizes, and prizes for all sorts of things, including the biggest deal, the smallest deal, the deal farthest from the office, the deal closest to the office, the first deal and the last deal. Mix it up. Use your imagination. Something for everybody all along the way. Avoid that ho-hum feeling that old so-and-so is obviously going to win so the hell with it. If you lose their interest, you lose your objective—production.

And stay away from cars as a prize. It leaves too much room for hanky-panky in the home stretch when a few points means the car or a bus ticket. Where do you think a real smarty would get those points? Now don't ask me to draw you a picture.

I heard of a guy who kept sales charts, month by month, showing the overall selling price of homes in his city. When the chart showed a two-month drop in prices, he showed it to vendors to help in getting the listing at the right price.

And when the chart showed a two-month rise in prices, he showed it to buyers, convincing them that now was the time to buy.

Got a drawing account? Do you realize that this can be a crutch, and a damaging factor in your career?

If you do not *absolutely* need a check a week from your broker, don't accept one. The danger with the damn thing is that you can actually relate your income to whatever amount is in the check, and nobody in real estate worth his salt should want to be satisfied with that!!

So you draw a couple of hundred a week and after six weeks you get a deal that closes in four, and your share is $2,000. Poof. No money. It all goes in the account, and you go on drawing your two bills a week. So you relate to $200 a week.

It would be much better if you could see the $2,000 all at once. Now, you are relating to paydays of $2,000, not $200.

A $2,000 check can inspire you to go on and get another one. The $200 check just inspires you to stick around for another.

If you don't need the weekly grocery money from the boss, leave it alone. Be independent. Ensure the checks *you* get are ones you have earned, and not those piddly little weekly draws.

So you have a salesman in your office who speaks Polish and three other languages. Good. How many fellow agents know about it? What's the big secret?

Check the staff. Make a list available for everybody indicating all languages spoken. Some day you will find yourself confronted by a language barrier, which could be quickly eliminated by one of your friendly "interpreters."

Here's what Bell Canada advises are highlights of good telephone usage:
- Answer promptly
- Identify yourself
- Establish your own communications island:
  a. have pad and pencil handy

    b. have a list of frequently called numbers
    c. have directories nearby
- Transfer calls properly
- Place and receive your own calls
- If you leave the line, explain why
- Leave a message when you leave your telephone
- Terminate calls courteously
- Always leave your telephone in capable hands

Bell Canada also has available a sixteen-page booklet called "Phone Tone." Write for it and help yourself to better use of one of the salesman's greatest money-makers of all time, the telephone.

You have your appointment book, but do you have a *business diary*? This is most important.

The business diary is a running account of what you did from day to day, including the commitments made to you, and commitments you have made to others.

In credibility, a business diary would carry more weight than an appointment book. One can add anything to a past-date page in an appointment book, but nothing can be added to a past-date in a running day-to-day diary simply because there is no room for the entry because of its continuity.

Start one now; you may find it very useful some day when you are called upon to substantiate a point, especially where it may affect your pocketbook.

Want to save a lot of time in preparing an offer to lease? Instead of outlining pages and pages of clauses, take the lessor's standard lease form and include it as part of the offer, with this clause: "It is understood and agreed that the lessor and lessee covenants will be as outlined in the lease form attached hereto." (The minor changes can be added to this in the offer.)

Besides patting your agents on the back when they produce good deals, back them up in other ways:

If anyone gets a hole-in-one, wins a bridge tournament, has an article published, gets on TV or radio, or does anything else of note, ensure that everyone is made aware of it. Believe it or not, there is more to life than money, and agents do recognize recognition. It will make you feel good for a whole day, and they just might go out and get themselves (and you) an extra deal.

Don't be cheap with your recognition.

When listing real estate, please do yourself a favor and *read the mortgage deeds.*

It would be most embarrassing (and possibly costly) for all concerned if an offer were accepted "cash to mortgages," only to discover at a later date that a mortgage deed contained a clause stipulating that if the fee is conveyed (property sold) the mortgage is to be paid off.

If someone asks you if he should pay off his mortgage or invest the money in something else, here's the answer:

What would the mortgagor do with the money if he didn't pay off the mortgage? Advise the person to estimate the annual return on an investment, less payable income tax.

Then, if what he receives is *less* than what his mortgage interest costs him, the mortgage should be paid off.

It is very easy to figure interest on the investment. Here is a reminder:

$$\text{Interest:} \quad \frac{742}{8,000} \quad \text{x} \quad \frac{100}{1} = 9.275\%$$
$$\text{Divided by principal:}$$

Want an extra deal or two a year?

Before you throw away that pile of old phone calls that got you nowhere, trade the pile for someone else's pile.

You have gone stale on your pile, and you're tired of them all. So start fresh. You call on a pile of old ones that will be new to you, and a fellow agent will call on your pile, which will be new ones to him. Sometimes it works wonders.

And if you are the sales manager, try this: Some night go through your agents' waste baskets and pick up all the discarded messages. Call them and introduce yourself. Believe it or not, people like to hear from the sales manager; they just might open up and give you some business.

And what a surprise and *lesson* it would be at your next sales meeting. (Don't embarrass the poor salesman. He'll be feeling bad enough without it).

———————

If you don't have mortgage conversion tables, and want to know the yield on a mortgage to be purchased, here you are:

Principal amount:	$5,500
Rate of interest:	11%
Simple annual return:	$605
Buying price:	$4,800

$$\frac{605}{4,800} \ \ x \ \ \frac{100}{1} = 12.6\% \text{ return}$$

———————

Here's a hot one. Once upon a time a broker received a letter on a fancy European letterhead. The writer said he was going to be in town in two weeks' time to invest a million or two, and would the broker please submit details of a few offerings to be scrutinized beforehand. It would save time you know!

The letterhead was a phony. It went to brokers all over town, and the replies were relayed to a broker-pal of the writer in the same city as the recipients of the letter. So now his pal knew more about what was available than anyone.

If you receive such a letter, get your bank manager to do a quick check on the writer before you give it all away. On one check the author did, the address was a cab stand in a mideast city, and the writer was a cab driver. Nice try fella.

43

Interest Rates

Remember, the more frequent the compounding, the greater the yield to the *lender*. The tables on the following pages will provide helpful information in determining interest calculations for a number of mortgage loans:

1) Interest-only loans
2) A fixed principal payment, plus interest
3) A blended payment (interest and principal)

The last column on each page shows the effective annual yield to the lender.

However, before calculating interest, ensure that you are familiar with the federal Interest Act, and its effect on mortgages. If you cannot obtain a copy locally, write to the Queen's Printer, Ottawa, Ontario, and get one.

Interest only loans: simply use the rate applicable to the compounding frequency and the period of payment.

Fixed principal payment, plus interest: On the first payment, use the appropriate rate for the entire amount of the loan. On subsequent payments, use the appropriate rate and apply it to the outstanding principal balance of the loan.

Blended payment (interest and principal): Calculate the interest using the appropriate rate. The payment will include interest and principal, so the balance of the payment will be the amount of principal to be deducted from the principal balance owing.

For example, a $10,000 loan, 10 per cent, compounded half-yearly, repayable $100 monthly. The first month's interest will be $81.64 on the $10,000, so the balance of the payment ($18.36) will be applied to the principal. Deduct this $18.36 from the $10,000 when estimating the second payment, so the interest on the second payment will be $9,981.64 x 0.816485, or $81.50. The balance of this month's payment of $100 will be $18.50, which will be applied to principal. Repeat this throughout the loan.

171

Compounded Monthly

	Payable Monthly	Payable Quarterly	Payable Semi-Annually	Payable Annually
10	0.833333	2.520891	5.105331	10.471307
10¼	0.845167	2.584450	5.235695	10.745514
10½	0.875000	2.648036	5.366192	11.020345
10¾	0.895833	2.711647	5.496825	11.295801
11	0.916667	2.775285	5.627592	11.571884
11¼	0.937500	2.838950	5.758496	11.848594
11½	0.958333	2.902640	5.889533	12.125933
11¾	0.979167	2.966357	6.020706	12.403901
12	1.000000	3.030100	6.152015	12.682503
12¼	1.020833	3.093869	6.283459	12.961736
12½	1.041667	3.157665	6.415039	13.241605
12¾	1.062500	3.221487	6.546754	13.522108
13	1.083333	3.285335	6.678605	13.803248
13¼	1.104167	3.349210	6.810592	14.085026
13½	1.125000	3.413111	6.942715	14.367444
13¾	1.145833	3.477038	7.074975	14.650502
14	1.166667	3.540992	7.207371	14.934203
14¼	1.187500	3.604972	7.339902	15.218546
14½	1.208333	3.668978	7.472571	15.503535
14¾	1.229167	3.733011	7.605375	15.789169
15	1.250000	3.797070	7.738318	16.075452
15¼	1.270833	3.861156	7.871397	16.362382
15½	1.291667	3.925267	8.004612	16.649962
15¾	1.312500	3.989406	8.137965	16.938195
16	1.333333	4.053570	8.271454	17.227078

Compounded Quarterly

	Payable Monthly	Payable Quarterly	Payable Semi-Annually	Payable Annually
10	0.826484	2.500000	5.062500	10.381289
10¼	0.846973	2.562500	5.190664	10.650758
10½	0.867453	2.625000	5.318906	10.920720
10¾	0.887930	2.687500	5.444723	11.191176
11	0.908390	2.750000	5.575625	11.462126
11¼	0.928846	2.812500	5.704102	11.733571
11½	0.949293	2.875000	5.832656	12.005511
11¾	0.969732	2.937500	5.961289	12.277947
12	0.990163	3.000000	6.090000	12.550881
12¼	1.010586	3.062500	6.218789	12.824311
12½	1.031001	3.125000	6.347656	13.098240
12¾	1.051407	3.187500	6.476602	13.372667
13	1.071805	3.250000	6.605625	13.647593
13¼	1.092194	3.312500	6.734727	13.923019
13½	1.112576	3.375000	6.863906	14.198945
13¾	1.132949	3.437500	6.993164	14.475372
14	1.153314	3.500000	7.122500	14.752300
14¼	1.176927	3.562500	7.272628	15.074166
14½	1.194020	3.625000	7.381406	15.307664
14¾	1.214360	3.687500	7.510976	15.586101
15	1.234693	3.750000	7.640625	15.865042
15¼	1.255017	3.812500	7.770351	16.144487
15½	1.275333	3.875000	7.900156	16.424437
15¾	1.295641	3.937500	8.030039	16.704893
16	1.315940	4.000000	8.160000	16.985856

Compounded Half-Yearly

	Payable Monthly	Payable Quarterly	Payable Semi-Annually	Payable Annually
10	0.816485	2.469508	5.000000	10.250000
10¼	0.836478	2.530483	5.125000	10.512656
10½	0.856452	2.591423	5.250000	10.775625
10¾	0.876405	2.652326	5.375000	11.038906
11	0.896338	2.713193	5.500000	11.302500
11¼	0.916254	2.774024	5.625000	11.566406
11½	0.936149	2.834819	5.750000	11.830625
11¾	0.956024	2.895578	5.875000	12.095156
12	0.975879	2.956301	6.000000	12.360000
12¼	0.995715	3.016989	6.125000	12.625156
12½	1.015532	3.077641	6.250000	12.890625
12¾	1.035329	3.138257	6.375000	13.156406
13	1.055107	3.198837	6.500000	13.422500
13¼	1.074866	3.259382	6.625000	13.688906
13½	1.094605	3.319892	6.750000	13.955625
13¾	1.114325	3.380366	6.875000	14.222656
14	1.134026	3.440804	7.000000	14.490000
14¼	1.153708	3.501208	7.125000	14.757656
14½	1.173370	3.561576	7.250000	15.025625
14¾	1.193013	3.621909	7.375000	15.293906
15	1.212679	3.682207	7.500000	15.562500
15¼	1.232243	3.742470	7.625000	15.831406
15½	1.251830	3.802697	7.750000	16.100625
15¾	1.271397	3.862890	7.875000	16.370156
16	1.290946	3.923048	8.000000	16.640000

Compounded Annually

	Payable Monthly	Payable Quarterly	Payable Semi-Annually	Payable Annually
10	0.797414	2.411369	4.880885	10.000000
10¼	0.816485	2.469508	5.000000	10.250000
10½	0.835516	2.527548	5.118980	10.500000
10¾	0.854507	2.585489	5.237826	10.750000
11	0.873459	2.643333	5.356538	11.000000
11¼	0.892372	2.701079	5.475115	11.250000
11½	0.911247	2.758727	5.593560	11.500000
11¾	0.930082	2.816279	5.711873	11.750000
12	0.948879	2.873734	5.830052	12.000000
12¼	0.967638	2.931094	5.948101	12.250000
12½	0.986358	2.988357	6.066017	12.500000
12¾	1.005040	3.045525	6.183803	12.750000
13	1.023684	3.102598	6.301458	13.000000
13¼	1.042291	3.159577	6.418983	13.250000
13½	1.060860	3.216461	6.536379	13.500000
13¾	1.079391	3.273252	6.653645	13.750000
14	1.097885	3.329948	6.770783	14.000000
14¼	1.116342	3.386552	6.887792	14.250000
14½	1.134762	3.443063	7.004673	14.500000
14¾	1.153145	3.499481	7.121426	14.750000
15	1.171492	3.555808	7.238053	15.000000
15¼	1.189801	3.612042	7.354553	15.250000
15½	1.208075	3.668185	7.470926	15.500000
15¾	1.226313	3.724237	7.587174	15.750000
16	1.244514	3.780199	7.703296	16.000000

44

Real Property Definitions

Abstract   A written, condensed history of title to a parcel of real property, recorded in a land registry office.

Abuttals   The bounding of a parcel of land by other land, street, river, etc. A boundary.

Acceleration clause   On mortgage payment default, the entire balance of the loan is due and immediately payable.

Administrator   One who has charge of the estate of a deceased person who died without a will, or one who did not appoint an executor. Appointed by court order.

Adverse possession   When someone, other than the owner, takes physical possession of property, without the owner's consent.

Agent   One who legally represents an individual or corporate body.

Agreement of sale   Written agreement whereby one agrees to buy, and another agrees to sell, according to the terms of the agreement.

Agreement to lease   Written agreement whereby one agrees to lease real property to another, according to the terms of the agreement.

Amortization   To extinguish a loan by means of a sinking fund.

Appraisal   A written estimate of the market value of real property, made by a qualified expert.

Appreciation   Increased market value of real property.

Appurtenances   Additional rights that are an adjunction to real property.

Assessed value	Value of real property set by a municipality for taxation purposes.
Assessor	Person employed by a municipality or other government body empowered to place valuation on property for taxation purposes.
Assignment	Legal transfer of interest in real property or a mortgage from one person to another.
Assumption agreement	An agreement whereby a person other than the mortgagor covenants to perform the obligations in the mortgage deed.
Attornment of rent	Taking of rents by mortgagee in possession to protect his rights in case of default by mortgagor.
Blanket mortgage	Single mortgage registered to cover more than one parcel of real property.
Bond	A binding agreement to strengthen the covenant of performance.
Broker	A person who legally trades in real estate for another, for compensation.
Certificate of charge	Provincial government acknowledgement of registration of mortgage in a land titles office.
Certificate of title	Provincial government acknowledgement of registration of title deed in a land titles office.
Chattels	Movable possessions, such as furniture, personal possessions, etc. A furnace, before it is installed, is a movable possession. Once installed, it is not.
Chattel mortgage	A mortgage on movable possessions, personal property.
Closing	The time at which a real estate transaction is concluded legally in a registry office.

Cloud on title An impairment to title of real property, such as executed judgment, mortgage, lien, etc., registered legally against the property.

C.M.H.C. Canada Mortgage and Housing Corporation, a Crown agency administering Canada's National Housing Act.

Commission Financial remuneration paid to an agent for selling or leasing property, based on an agreed percentage of the amount involved.

Consideration Something of value for compensation.

Contract An agreement upon lawful consideration which binds the parties to a performance.

Conveyance Transmitting title of real property from one to another.

Covenant Solemn agreement.

Covenantee Lender in a (mortgage) deed.

Covenantor Borrower in a (mortgage) deed.

Date of maturity In mortgages, the last day of the term of the mortgage.

Deed A document containing an agreement that has been signed, sealed and containing proof of its delivery; effective only on the date of delivery. (Mortgage deed, title deed, etc.)

Demise To transfer or convey an estate for a term of years, or life.

Deposit Money or other consideration of value given as pledge for fulfillment of a contract or agreement.

Depreciation Reduction in market value of property. Also used to indicate capital cost allowance.

Derivative mortgage	Mortgage on a mortgage. Mortgagee assigns his mortgage to lender to secure loan.
Dower	Rights of wife or widow in freehold property owned by her husband.
Easement	A right acquired to use another's land or buildings, generally for access to some other adjoining property.
Encroachment	Undue or unlawful trespass on another's property, usually caused by a building, or part of a building, or obstruction.
Encumbrance	Any legal claim registered against property.
Escheat	Conveyance of property to the Crown due to intestate person dying and leaving no heirs.
Escrow	A deed or contract delivered to a third party to be held until the payment or fulfillment of the agreement by the grantee.
Estate	One's interest in lands and any other subject of property.
Equity	The financial interest of a property owner in excess of any encumbrances, limited by its market value.
Executor	Person legally appointed by testator to carry out the terms of his/her will.
Exclusive listing	An agreement granting sole and exclusive rights to an agent to sell property.
Fee simple	Absolute ownership of property.
Fee tail	Property ownership, limited to some particular heirs.
First mortgage	One that takes precedence over all others. (Mortgage seniority established by date and time of registration.)

Fixture Permanent improvements to property that remain with it.

Foreclosure A legally enforced transfer of real property ordered by a court to satisfy unpaid debts. The most common is a foreclosure by a mortgagee.

Freehold Property held in fee simple (untrammelled tenure) or fee tail (for the term of the owner's life.)

Frontage Property line facing street.

Gale date The date on which interest is charged.

Grant An instrument of conveyance transferring property from one to another.

Grantee Person to whom a conveyance is made; one who receives legal transfer of property from another; the buyer.

Grantor Person who makes a conveyance; one who transfers property to another; the seller.

Hereditament Property that may be inherited.

Hypothec Lien on real estate (Quebec).

Hypothecary creditor Mortgagee (Quebec).

Hypothecary debtor Mortgagor (Quebec).

Indenture An agreement between two or more parties. Originally, indentures were duplicates placed together and cut in a wavy line, so that the two papers could be identified as being authentic by corresponding to each other.

Instrument A writing instructing one in regard to something that has been agreed on.

Intestate Not having a will.

Joint tenancy	Ownership of real property by two or more persons; when one dies, that share automatically passes to the survivor(s).
Judgment	Binding decision of the court.
Landed property	Having an interest in and pertaining to the land.
Landlord	A lessor. One who allows another to occupy his/her land or building for a consideration.
Lease	Binding contract between a landlord (lessor) and tenant (lessee) for the occupation of premises or land for a specified period of time, and a financial or other consideration.
Leasehold	Property held by lease.
Leaseholder	Tenant under a lease.
Lessee	The tenant. One who pays rent.
Lessor	The person granting use of property to another.
Lien	A legal claim affecting property.
Lis pendens	Notice of commencement of court action, recorded against title of property.
Market value	The courts have defined this as being the highest price estimated in terms of money which a property will bring, if exposed for sale in the open market, allowing a reasonable time to find a purchaser who buys with knowledge of all the uses to which it may be put, and for which it is capable of being used.
Mechanic's lien	A lien filed and registered against property by a person or corporate body, for labor and/or materials supplied for the improvement of the property.

Moratorium	Provincial statute deferment of mortgage principal payments during depression. Nonexistent now.
Mortgage	A deed given to lender to secure a debt by a borrower. In Quebec, a lien on an immovable.
Mortgage bonds	Bond holders are represented by a trustee, who is the mortgagee. Bonds can be traded, making them more flexible than individual mortgages.
Mortgaged out	Situation whereby total mortgage debt on property equals or exceeds market value of property.
Mortgagee	The lender in a mortgage deed. The one receiving the mortgage.
Mortgagor	The borrower in a mortgage deed. The one giving the mortgage.
N.H.A.	National Housing Act.
Option	An agreement whereby one has the exclusive right to purchase another's property at a specified price, with a time limit.
Personalty	Personal property, chattels.
Postponement clause	In mortgaging, the agreement of an equitable mortgagee to allow the mortgagor to renew or replace a senior mortgage that becomes due before such equitable mortgage.
Power of attorney	Legal authority for one to act on behalf of another.
Prepayment clause	In a mortgage, an agreement giving the mortgagor the privilege of paying additional sums off the principal balance over and above the agreed payments.
Principal	A person or corporate body employing an agent.

Principal balance	In a mortgage, the outstanding dollar amount owing on the debt.
Quit claim deed	A full release of one's interest in property to another, usually executed between mortgagees and mortgagors.
Real estate	Landed property (land).
Real property	Land *and* buildings thereon, and rights thereof.
Realtor	Certification mark being the property of the Canadian Real Estate Association. Designates broker-member of Association.
Realty	Real property.
Rest	The date upon which the amount between the parties to a mortgage is altered. It is not necessarily the date upon which payment is made, unless so agreed in the mortgage deed.
Sales agreement	Purchase of property without obtaining title deed until a specified further sum of money is paid to the vendor.
Socage	A tenure of land held by the tenant in performance of specified services or by payment of rent, and not requiring military service (history).
Straight loan	In mortgaging, a mortgage with no principal payments. Interest only.
Survey	Surveyor's report of mathematical boundaries of land, showing location of buildings, physical features and quantity of land.
Tenancy in common	Ownership of real property by two or more persons, whereby on the death of one, that share is credited to his/her own estate.
Tenant	The one who pays rent for the right to occupy land or buildings.

Tenant in tail   Holder of an estate limited to the heirs of his/her body. The line of heirs is called entail.

Tenement   Property held by tenant.

Tenure   The right of holding property

Title deed   Proof of legal ownership of property.

Title search   Research of records in registry or land titles office to determine history and chain or ownership of property.

Usury   An unconscionable and exorbitant rate of interest.

Zoning   Specified limitation on the use of land, the construction and use of buildings, in a defined section of a municipality.

45

Building Definitions

Canada Mortgage and Housing Corporation has provided us with a comprehensive list of building terms in construction, including the areas of electricity, heating, plumbing and the roof.

Construction Types

Adobe A type of construction in which the exterior walls are built of blocks that are made of soil mixed with straw and hardened in the sun.

Block A type of construction in which the exterior walls are bearing walls made of concrete block or structural clay tile.

Brick A type of construction in which the exterior walls are bearing walls made of brick or a combination of brick and other unit masonry.

Brick-veneer A type of construction in which the wood frame or steel structural frame has an exterior surface of brick applied as cladding.

Dry-wall Interior cladding with panels of gypsum board, fibre board, plywood or gypsum plaster, a dry operation as opposed to wet plaster.

Fire resistive Floors, walls, roof, etc., constructed of slow-burning or noncombustible materials recognized as such by building codes or local regulations applicable to the type of building proposed.

Monolithic concrete A type of construction or process in which the concrete for the wall, floor, beams, etc. are poured in one continuous operation.

Plank frame A type of construction in which the structural framework is composed of solid wood plank uprights and horizontally placed planks laid on edge, with or without sheathing.

Post and beam A type of construction made with load-bearing posts and beams in which the enclosing walls are designed to support no loads other than their own weight.

Prefabricated A type of construction so designed as to involve a minimum of assembly at the site, usually comprising a series of large wood panels or precast concrete units manufactured in a plant.

Reinforced concrete A type of construction in which the principal structural members, such as floors, columns and beams are made of concrete poured around isolated steel bars or steel meshwork in such a manner that the two materials act together in resisting force.

Skeleton A type of construction in which all external and internal loads and stresses are transmitted to the foundations by a rigidly connected framework of metal or reinforced concrete. The enclosing walls are supported by the frame at designated intervals, usually at each storey.

Steel frame A type of construction in which the structural parts are of steel or dependent on a steel frame for support.

Wood frame or frame A type of construction in which the structural parts are wood or dependent upon a wood frame for support. In codes, if brick or other incombustible material is applied to exterior walls, the classification of this type of construction is usually unchanged.

Electrical Terms

Alternating current	A flow of current which constantly changes direction at a fixed rate.
Ampere	A measure of electric current.
Cable: armored cable	Insulated wire having additional flexible metallic protective sheathing—often referred to as BX cable.
Ceiling outlet	An outlet for ceiling lighting fixtures.
Circuit	Continuous conducting path through which current flows.
Circuit breaker	An automatic mechanical device which serves the same purpose as a fuse, i.e., to prevent overheating in a circuit through overloading.
Conduit	A protective, pipelike covering for electrical wiring.
Convenience outlet	An outlet into which may be plugged portable equipment, such as lamps or electrically operated equipment.
Current	A flow of electricity.
Direct current	A flow of current constantly in one direction.
Fuse	A device for interupting an electric circuit under conditions of overloading or short circuiting, comprising a fusible element which fuses at predetermined excess loads so as to open the circuit.
Insulation	Nonconducting covering applied to wire or equipment to prevent the flow of current to contiguous materials.
Kilowatt hour	A unit of measurement of the consumption of electric energy at a fixed rate for one hour; specifically, the use of 1,000 watts for one hour.

Meter	A device used for measuring the amount of electric energy consumed.
Outlet	A point on an electric circuit designed for the direct connection of lighting fixtures, appliances and equipment.
Panelboard	A center for controlling a number of circuits by means of fuses or circuit breakers, usually contained in a metal cabinet. Switches are sometimes added to control each circuit.
Power circuit	A circuit transmitting electric energy to a motor or a heating unit too large to be served by an ordinary circuit.
Radio outlet	An outlet having connected thereto an aerial and ground for the use of a radio.
Special purpose outlet	An outlet used for purposes other than ordinary lighting and power.
Switch	A device to open and close a circuit.
Three-way switch	A switch designed to operate in conjunction with a similar switch to control one outlet from two points.
Transformer	A device for transforming the voltage characteristics of a current supply.
Voltage	A measure of electric pressure between any two wires of an electric circuit.
Watt	A unit of measurement of electric power.
Wiring: knob-and-tube	A method of exposed wiring using knobs and tubes of nonconducting materials to insulate the wiring from the surfaces on which or through which it is installed.

Heating Terms

Air conditioning	The process of bringing air to a required state of temperature and humidity, and removing dust, pollen and other foreign matter.

Baseboard heaters	A radiator shaped like a regular, decorative baseboard, but having openings at top and bottom through which air circulates. Provides convected and radiant heat.
Conduction	The transfer or travel of heat through a body by molecular action.
Convector	Having removable front. Air enters through the arched opening near the floor, is heated as it passes through the heating element and enters room through the upper grill.
Hot water heating	The circulation of hot water through a system of pipes and radiators either by gravity or a circulating pump.
Indirect heating	A system of heating by convection.
Panel heating	Coils or ducts installed in wall, floor, or ceiling panels to provide a large surface of low intensity heat supply.
Panel radiator	A heating unit place on or flush with a flat wall surface, and intended to function essentially as a radiator.
Radiant heating	A heating system in which only the heat radiated from panels is effective in providing the heating requirements.
Radiation	The transfer of heat from a substance by the emission of heat waves.
Radiator	The part of the system, exposed or concealed, from which heat is radiated to a room or other space within the building; heat transferring device.
Space heating	The methods of heating individual rooms or living units by equipment located entirely within these rooms or living units, such equipment consisting of single unit without ducts, piping, or other

mechanical means of heat distribution exterior to the room in which situated.

Steam heating   The circulation of steam through a system of pipes and radiators by any of the numerous methods employed.

Two-pipe system   A heating system in which one pipe is used for the supply of the heating medium to the heating unit and another for the return of the heating medium to the source of heat supply. The essential feature of a two-pipe system is that each heating unit receives a direct supply of the heating medium which cannot have served a preceding heating unit.

Warm air heating   A warm air heating plant consists of a heating unit (fuel-burning furnace) enclosed in a casing, from which the heated air is distributed to various rooms of the building through ducts.

Warm air heating, forced   A warm air heating system in which circulation of air is effected by a fan. Such a system includes air cleaning devices.

Warm air heating, gravity   A warm air heating system in which the motive heat producing flow depends on the difference in weight between the heated air leaving the casing and the cooler air entering the bottom of the casing.

Warm air heating, perimeter   A warm air heating system of the combination panel and convection type. Warm air ducts embedded in the concrete slab of a basementless house, around the perimeter, receive heated air from a furnace and deliver it to the heated space through registers placed in or near the floor. Air is returned to the furnace from registers near the ceiling.

Plumbing Terms

Backflow

The flow of water into a water supply system from any source except its regular one. Back siphonage is one type of back-flow.

Building drainage system

All piping provided for carrying waste water, sewage or other drainage, from the building to the street sewer or place of disposal.

Building subdrain

That portion of a drainage system which cannot drain by gravity into the building sewer.

Building main

The water supply pipe, including fittings and accessories, from the water (street) main or other source of supply to the first branch of the water distributing system.

Catch basin

A small underground structure for surface drainage in which sediment may settle before water reaches the drain lines.

Cesspool

A covered pit with open-jointed linings into which raw sewage is discharged, the liquid portion of which is disposed of by seepage or leaching into the surrounding porous soil, the solids or sludge being retained in the pit.

Downspout

A pipe which carries water from the roof or gutter to the ground or to any part of the drainage system (synonymous with the conductor, leader, rainspout).

Dry well

A covered pit with open-jointed linings through which drainage from roofs, base-ment floors or areaways may seep or leach into the surrounding porous soil.

Dual main system

The use of two underground conduits, pipes or lines, each to supply water to one side of a street.

Main   The principal artery of the system to which branches may be connected.

Fixtures   Receptacles which receive and discharge water, liquid or water-borne wastes into a drainage system with which they are connected.

Plumbing stack   A general term for the vertical main of a system of soil, waste or vent piping.

Plumbing system   A system of pipes including the water service line and building drainage lines from their several connections within the building to their connections with the public mains or individual water supply and sewage disposal systems, together with fixtures, traps, vents and other devices connected thereto. Storm water drainage pipes may be considered a part of the plumbing system when connected to a public sewage system.

Roughing-in   The work of installing all pipes in the drainage and venting systems and all water pipes to the point where connections are made with the plumbing fixtures.

Septic tank   A sewage settling tank intended to retain the sludge in immediate contact with the sewage flowing through the tank, for a sufficient period to secure satisfactory decomposition of organic sludge solids by bacterial action.

Sewage   The liquid or water-borne wastes carried away from buildings with or without such ground or surface water as may be present.

Sewer   A conduit, usually closed, designed or used for carrying sewage from buildings and/or ground and surface water to sewage disposal plants or to natural bodies of water.

| Sewer system | A system comprising all sewers (sanitary, storm, and combined), culverts, and sub-surface drains needed to conduct sanitary sewage and storm water from a site. |

Sewer Types

| Building sewer | That part of the horizontal piping of a building drainage system extending from the building drain to the street sewer or other place of disposal (a cesspool, septic tank or other type of sewage-treatment device or devices) and conveying the drainage of but one building site. |

| Sanitary sewer | A sewer designed or used only for conveying liquid or water-borne waste from plumbing fixtures. |

| Storm sewer | A sewer used for conveying rain or subsurface water. |

| Sewerage | The composite parts of a sewer system, including conduits, pumping stations, treatment works and such other works as may be employed in the collection, treatment or disposal of sewage. |

| Soil pipe | Any pipe that conveys the discharges of water-closets, or fixtures having similar functions, with or without the discharges from other fixtures. |

| Tile field | The system of open-joint drain tiles laid to distribute septic tank effluent over its absorption area. A tile system laid to provide subsoil drainage for wet areas. |

| Trap | A fitting or device so designed and constructed as to provide a liquid trap seal which will prevent the passage of air through it. |

| Vent | A pipe installed to provide a flow of air to or from a drainage system or to provide a |

circulation of air within such system to protect trap seals from siphonage and back pressure.

Vent Types

Bank vent

A branch vent installed primarily for the purpose of protecting fixture traps from self-siphonage.

Vent stack

A vertical vent pipe installed primarily for the purpose of providing circulation of air to and from any part of the building drainage system.

Water closet

A plumbing fixture consisting of a bowl for the reception of fecal discharge and equipment for flushing the bowl with water. A minor enclosed space in a building equipped with such plumbing fixture.

Water distribution system

All water mains and service lines, outside of building lines (or to a point near the building line), needed for domestic water supply and fire protection.

Water supply system

All the water service pipes, the water distributing pipes, and the necessary connecting pipes fittings and control valves.

Roof Types

Curb (or curbed)

A roof in which the slope is broken on two or more sides; so called because a horizontal curb is built at the plane where the slope changes.

Deck

Having sloping sides below and a flat deck on top.

Flat

A roof which is flat or one which is pitched only enough to provide drainage.

Flat-pitch

A roof with only a moderately sloping surface.

Gabled	A ridge roof which terminates in a gable.
Gambrel	A gable roof each slope of which is broken into two planes.
Hip	In general, a roof which has one or more hips. A roof which has four sloping sides that meet at four hips and a ridge.
Lean-to	A roof which has a single sloping surface that is supported at the top by a wall that is higher than the roof. A roof which has a single sloping surface.
Mansard	A type of curb roof in which the pitch of the upper portion of a sloping side is slight and that of the lower portion steep. The lower portion is usually interrupted by dormer windows.
Monitor	A type of gable roof commonly used on industrial buildings, which has a raised portion along the ridge with openings for light and/or air.
Pavilion	A roof which in plan forms a figure of more than four straight sides.
Pent	A roof, other than a lean-to roof, which has a single sloping surface.
Pitched	A roof which has one or more sloping surfaces pitched at angles greater than necessary for drainage.
Polygonal	A roof which in plan forms a figure bounded by more than four straight lines.
Pyramid	A hip roof which has four sloping surfaces, usually of equal pitch, that meet at a peak.
Ridge	A roof which has one or more ridges.
Shed	A roof with only one set of rafters, falling from a higher to a lower wall, like an aisle roof.